Ledyard Bill

The History of Paxton, Massachusetts

Ledyard Bill

The History of Paxton, Massachusetts

ISBN/EAN: 9783743411012

Manufactured in Europe, USA, Canada, Australia, Japa

Cover: Foto ©ninafisch / pixelio.de

Manufactured and distributed by brebook publishing software
(www.brebook.com)

Ledyard Bill

The History of Paxton, Massachusetts

THE

HISTORY OF PAXTON,

MASSACHUSETTS.

BY LEDYARD BILL,

AUTHOR OF "A WINTER IN FLORIDA," "CLIMATES FOR INVALIDS," AND A WORK ON "GENEALOGY."

WORCESTER, MASS.:
PUBLISHED BY PUTNAM, DAVIS & CO.
1889.

Entered according to Act of Congress in 1889,
By LEDYARD BILL,
In the Office of the Librarian of Congress in Washington.

PREFACE.

This volume is the outcome of an engagement with the publishers of the History of this County, to furnish a sketch of Paxton for that work. Having finished the undertaking with them, and believing that the citizens of the town would kindly welcome any effort on the part of any one to rescue from oblivion interesting data, whether skillfully set forth or otherwise, we concluded to prepare for publication in a separate volume the material supplied for the work above named, together with such additions as seemed essential to greater completeness.

Of course, a much larger volume than this might easily have been made, more easily than otherwise, in fact, and perhaps all in all proved more satisfactory. We have, however, endeavored to embrace within these pages the essential facts, and any enlargement would have involved, not only a greater labor of love, but an increased cost, which, in view of all the circumstances would not be justified.

It is to be regretted that a volume of this character had not been undertaken at an earlier period, and by other hands, and thereby much of special interest that is now lost to us might have been preserved, since within the past few years several aged people who had treasured up a great store of anecdote and incident, have passed away. Had we even dreamed of this task falling to our lot, we should have eagerly garnered much of the now lost material.

Finally, this brief volume is submitted with its many imperfections to the people of whom it treats, believing they will excuse all errors and omissions, and exercise that charity which is demanded in the premises and which much of historical statement seems to require.

In the mention of families, we have for the most part confined ourselves to such as were long resident here, or have had some prominence, and thus connected themselves with the history of the town.

L. B.

Paxton, Mass., Feb. 14, 1889.

THE HISTORY OF PAXTON.

IF lines were drawn diagonally across the Commonwealth, from and to each of its four corners, the point of crossing would be within, or nearly so, the borders of the little town of Paxton; hence it might be truly said, speaking geographically, that this town is the "axis" of the State, and that the high point of land known as Asnebumskit Mountain is the "hub" itself; thus may the least of towns aspire to rival, in some senses, the greatest!

This town lies about fifty-five miles west of Boston, and some seven miles from the city of Worcester, and is bounded and described as follows, namely: On the north by Rutland, on the east by Holden and Worcester, on the south by Leicester, and on the west by Spencer and Oakham. The town is situated upon high and rugged lands, and belongs to that class of towns known as the "hill towns" of the State. The general elevation above tide-water would not be very far from eleven hundred feet; indeed, the village "common" is, to be tolerably exact, eleven hundred and thirty-five feet above the sea, while the southernmost spur of the White Mountain range, Asnebumskit, is about fourteen hundred feet above water level, and is, with the exception of Mount Wachusett, the highest land lying east of the Connecticut River. The land surface is not so broken and irregular as might be inferred from its considerable elevation, but is rather a succession of rounded hills on which are situated some of the best of farming lands and farms, and again the valleys stretch away, here and there, into level tracts both fertile and pleasant, and between the hills and valleys of this town are found many thrifty homes and a comparatively contented population.

This town does not rank among the ancient corporations, but yet it has passed its first century, and may be said to have seen "generations come and go." The reasons which moved the early settlers to ask to be incorporated were various, but chief among those they gave in their petition was " the great difficulties they labored under in attending public worship, in consequence of the great distance they were from its places in the towns to which they belong." The foregoing petition was presented to the Legislature in 1761, and was unsuccessful, as nearly every petition of this nature is apt to be on its first presentation.

The people thus petitioning for a separate municipality were citizens of Leicester and Rutland, and the tract of land desired by the petitioners was that portion of the two towns lying contiguous, viz.: the southern part of Rutland and the northern portion of Leicester, making a tract of about four miles square. They complained in their first petition and subsequent appeals to the General Court that the distance to places of worship was great, and doubtless the same reason held good when it came to the transaction of the business of the two towns, since the centre of each of these towns was full five miles distant, and we can well imagine the condition of the highways in those early days, when the best were but very indifferent roads, while the side-ways were mere bridle-paths, making it quite a task in the inclement season to perform those public duties incumbent upon them.

The inhabitants, however, had the merit of persistency, and the following year they again petitioned and were again rejected; but nothing daunted, they still worked for the accomplishment of their final purpose; so in 1763, feeling, doubtless, the inconvenience of their position more and more, they again renewed their importunities and received some support from one of the towns, but the other (Rutland) opposing, the case was still deferred.

The following petition was presented to the authorities of Leicester by the undersigned, and this town, at a town meeting held on May 16, 1763, voted affirmatively on the petition, which was the first favorable action looking towards the establishment of the new town:

To the Selectmen of the town of Leicester, and the other inhabitants of the same:

The petition and desire of the subscribers hereof humbly showeth,— That whereas, in the government of Divine Providence, our inhabitants are at a great distance from the place of public worship in this town, which, together with the snow and moisture of the land, it is exceedingly difficult, a great part of the year, to attend on the public worship of God in this town; We look upon it as our bounden duty to endeavor to set up the Gospel among us, by which we, with our families, might more constantly enjoy its means of grace.

In order to accomplish the good end of setting up the Gospel, we propose, if possible to obtain leave so to do, to erect a town or district between the towns of Leicester and Rutland, by taking two miles off each town to make up the contents of four square miles. Wherefore your petitioners humbly and earnestly desire that, for the good end above proposed, you would now sett off, by a vote of this town, two miles at the north end of this town, the lands with the inhabitance thereon, to be laid out and connected with the south part of Rutland that is adjoining the same, to be erected into a town or district by order of the Great and General Court of this province, as soon as may be, that we may set up a Congregational Church and settle a gospel minister, according to the constitution of the churches in the land ; which we judge will be for the advancement of religion and our comfort if it be obtained in the way of peace. So wishing your health and peace, as in duty bound, we subscribe your petitioners:

Leicester, May 13, 1763.

Oliver Witt,	James Thompson,
Timothy Barrett,	William Thompson, Jr.,
Abraham Smith,	Abijah Bemis,
Abner Morse,	Daniel Snow, Jr.,
William Thompson,	James Nichol,
Jason Livermore,	Isaac Bellows,
Nathan Livermore,	Daniel Steward.

Finally a fourth attempt was made by these people, and the petition this time headed by one Oliver Witt, followed by many others, was duly presented to the Legislature, and this time with better results, for it was ordered " that Jedediah Foster, of Brookfield, and Col. Williams, on the part of the House, and Benjamin Lincoln, of the Council, be a committee in the recess of this court to repair to the place petitioned for to be erected into a parish, at the charge of the petitioners, and that they hear all parties interested for and against said corporation, and report at the next session whether the prayer thereof should be granted."

This committee held several meetings, at which there were hearings of all the parties interested, and at the succeeding session of the General Court reported, on June 23, 1765, a bill entitled, "An Act for Incorporating the Southerly part of Rutland and the Northerly part of Leicester, in the county of Worcester, into a District by the name of Paxton." This bill, after brief reference to the appropriate committee, was reported back to the full house and speedily passed both branches of the General Court, and received Governor Francis Bernard's signature on the 12th of February, Anno Domini 1765. Thus was the frail bark of Paxton duly launched, possessing all the rights, privileges and immunities of any other town, except the right to send a representative on its sole account, but gave the right to "join with the town of Leicester and the precinct of Spencer" in choosing a representative to the Legislature.

It is proper to make some reference to the name given the town by the act of incorporation, and perhaps no better account can be given than the following, which has come under our observation, viz.: "When the bill for incorporating this town passed the House of Representatives no name was inserted; the blank was filled in the Council by the word Paxton, in honor of Charles Paxton, who at that time was marshal of the Admiralty Court and a friend and favorite of Francis Bernard, the Governor, and of Thomas Hutchison, the Deputy-Governor. It is said that Paxton promised the town a church-bell if it was named for him; this promise was never fulfilled. Charles Paxton, although polished in manners and of pleasing address, was an intriguing politician and a despicable sycophant; 'every man's humble servant, but no man's friend,' as his paper figure was labeled, when, on Pope's day, as the anniversary of the gunpowder plot was called, it was paraded through the streets of Boston standing between the effigies of the Pope and the devil. He was the tool of Charles Townsend, the Chancellor of the English Exchequer, and with him devised the scheme of raising a revenue from the colonies by a tax on glass, paper, painter's colors and tea. The passage of this bill by the Parliament of England was greatly aided by Paxton, and returning to Boston, he was put at the head of this internal tax system, and made himself especially obnoxious to the people by reason of his issuing search-warrants to discover supposed smuggled goods, and his course was so insolent and tyrannical that he became an object of public hatred, was even hung in effigy upon Liberty Tree, and was subsequently, by the wrath of the people, driven into Castle William, and finally, at the evacuation, he departed with the British troops and went to England, where he died in 1788."

The course of this man, who had christened the town with his own name, was such that the bad odor of it reached the inhabitants of the newly-fledged district and they were intensely disgusted, and among the earlier public acts of the citizens was to petition for a change of name, and why the Legislature did not grant this reasonable request is a marvel. It should be attempted even at this late day, and there is no good reason why a new name would not be readily granted.

There have been several additions at sundry times

to the territory of Paxton. At one time, on the petition of John Davis, Ebenezer Boynton, Nathan Harrington, Samuel Harrington, Micah Harrington and Ephraim Harrington, of Holden, their estates were set off from Holden on February 13, 1804, and attached to the town of Paxton, and, by this act, the town line was extended so as to border on Worcester. Still another addition from Holden was made in April, 1839. Again, in 1851, a small strip was added from the same source, and there is still room for improving the present zig-zag boundary line between Holden and Paxton. The total acreage is now about eight thousand five hundred acres. The population of Paxton at the time of incorporation is not known, but it is presumed to "have been some hundreds," says an unknown writer in the *Worcester Magazine*, published a half-century or more ago. It is quite likely that the settlement of this portion of the country was well under way the latter part of the first century after the landing of the Pilgrims. It was, indeed, about 1720 that Rutland was incorporated and Leicester settled, and all this region of country taken up gradually by natural gravitation of the population westward, this section being at that period of time the "great west," and had its border-wars and conflicts with the aborigines and their allies. Doubtless there were wise men in those days who were wont to say to the wayward and the self-aspiring in the crowded centres of population along the seaboard : "Go west, young man, go west." And so, in the lapse of time, these hill-towns, with those in the valleys, have filled up and the great army of emigrants has continued from that day to this to flow westward, founding new States, enlarging the boundaries of civilization and establishing both law and liberty, on firm foundations, over a vast territory.

Thus these hill-towns, so despised in the eyes of some ephemeral writers who draw distressing pictures of "abandoned farms, dwindling villages, decayed meeting-houses, diminished schools and poor highways," have contributed largely to the public weal.

The marvelous strides this country has made in the last century are chiefly by reason of the inexhaustible supply of men and women drawn from the hills and valleys of New England, where they have been trained in the schools of industry and frugality. These have given direction and force to the upbuilding of the great region of the West. Thus, while it is true that the populations of the hill-towns, with some of those even in the valleys here in New England, have diminished, the cause is not permanently disturbing—since the era of cheap lands is about closing and the reflex tide cannot be far distant when New England will be filled to overflowing, and then this assumed prophecy of a premature decay will have been forgotten. The country is to be taken as a whole and not judged by any of its minor members.

The statement that there "were some hundreds" of people in the district of Paxton at the time of incorporation could hardly have meant more than two or three hundred at the most, for in 1790 the number was but 558; in 1820 it rose to 613 and in 1850 to 870, while in 1880 it had fallen to 592, and in 1885 the State census gave the town only 561.

The population in 1870 was, we believe, well towards nine hundred, but, in part owing to the destruction of one of the chief industries by fire, which, unfortunately, was never re-established, it has gradually fallen to a point in numbers to about what it was one hundred years ago.

The town is at the present time purely agricultural, there being no manufacturing of any description carried on here.

In former years the boot and shoe industry was the principal business, or, at least, monopolized a very great share of the attention of the people; and the product of the shops was equal, if it did not greatly exceed in value the products of all the farms in town.

In 1820 John Partridge established the boot business in Paxton, and continued in the same line to the time of his decease, which occurred some fifteen years since, having been in business over half a century. The next notable firm to follow in the same line of industry was that of Messrs. Lakin & Bigelow, and they were succeeded by R. E. Bigelow & Son. All of these parties accumulated quite large fortunes, but none of their descendants reside within the town at the present time.

The town of Paxton is so situated, and has such natural beauty of landscape, and from its summits such extended and charming views of the surrounding country, that its ultimate destiny is by no means uncertain. Already many scores of visitors rest here during the summer months, and annually come back to "view the landscape o'er" and breathe again the wholesome and health invigorating air of these primeval hills and valleys. From the top of Asnebumskit, on a clear day, a score of towns may be seen, and from its summit a fine bird's-eye view of the city of Worcester can be obtained, which alone well repays the tourist for all his labors. There is still another eminence, known as Crocker Hill; this swell of land lies a few rods east of the village, and from the top there is a fine view of Wachusett, also of Monadnock and the Hoosac Mountains. This point is a charming spot to all who have any taste for the beautiful in nature. The wonder is, that some capitalist does not secure it, pitch his tent on the same and invite the world to dine with him and spend all of the "midsummer nights" at this breezy and delightful place. On "Christian Hill," west of the village church, is another landscape to the northward which is unsurpassed for quiet loveliness. Some day an artist will *discover* it, and it will then be famous for its exceeding beauty.

It may be thought unusual for elevated lands to hold many ponds or lakes; but, however that may be, Paxton has a goodly supply, inasmuch as there are some half a dozen artificial or natural ponds within the town's boundaries.

Of these, Lake Asnebumskit is by far the most interesting. This is located at the northern slope of the mountain whose name it bears, and covers, perhaps, sixty acres, "more or less," as the legal phrase is. It is elliptical in form and has an average depth of perhaps seven feet. All the sources of supply for this attractive sheet of water come from the springs in and around it. These springs are uniformly cold and clear; especially is this true of one at the southern shore, near the present carriage-way to the lake. The outlet is at the extreme northern end, and the flow is considerable. It supplies the Haggett Pond, and in its rapid descent furnishes power for Harrington's grist-mill, planing-mill and saw-mill, and then turns abruptly eastward, flowing through Holden, and on to the Quinepoxet and Nashua Rivers, and thus to the sea.

This lake has been famed for its fine pickerel and perch, and for many years afforded most excellent fishing for many people far and near. Latterly, however, its supply diminished, and some dozen years ago a few citizens formed a club and, securing a lease from the Commonwealth, stocked it with black-bass, and these were left for several years to increase, but when fishing was recommenced it was discovered that the bass had destroyed the most of the native fish, and, as many of the bass made their escape through the lake's outlet, little headway was made in stocking the pond. The club subsequently relinquished to the town all their rights, whereupon the town took out a lease, and all have the old-time privilege restored, but the fish are not plentiful in the lake at this time.

Bottomly Pond is the largest body of water in the town. It is about one mile in length, has irregular shores, and is of varying width, while its depth must average ten feet or more. It is for the most part an artificial pond, and is used as a storage-pond for the mills below, of which there are quite a number.

This pond lies just south of the village and west of the Worcester and Paxton county road, but only the southern end is in view from the highway mentioned. It is there that the joke concerning the "Paxton Navy-Yard" was perpetrated, which is so frequently mentioned even to this day. It was some years ago, and in the late autumn, as the stage-coach with its complement of passengers reached this place in the highway (Arnold's Mill), where there was afforded a tolerable view of the lake. A sailor passenger, who had at least "three sheets in the wind," on gazing out and seeing the forest trees at the left, with their bare trunks and branches in close proximity to the water, recalled his wandering senses sufficiently to exclaim "Is—hic—this —hic—the navy-yard?" The solemn quiet which had prevailed with the passengers in the coach up to this time was suddenly broken. The ludicrous remark, and the very absurdity of the whole subject, as applied to a section of country twelve hundred feet above tide-water and fifty miles inland, and coming, too, from a furloughed sailor just off ship, was too much, and all, as it were, "tumbled" to the same, and the joke seems ever fresh in the mouths of men inclined to poke a little fun.

Turkey Hill Pond is a natural body of water near the Barre county road, about two miles north of the centre of the town. It is perhaps a fourth of a mile in width. Its waters are dark and the fishing is fair, though not nearly as good as in former years. The outlet is at the southern extremity, and forms what was once known as Jennison's Brook, crossing the highway near what is now known as the "town-farm," and empties into Comins' mill-pond, formerly Jennison's mill-pond, and thence southwesterly through Spencer and the Brookfields to the Chicopee River. Formerly there was at the outlet of this pond a fulling-mill and carding-factory.

There are several small streams flowing into this Jennison Brook within the limits of the town. One of these rises in the southwesterly part of Rutland, passes into Paxton, and unites with the brook above named in the meadow below Comins's mill. Another rises about five hundred yards southeast of the meeting house, on lands owned by the late John Partridge, and flows southerly across the village farm of the writer into Lakin's meadow and thence northwesterly to Howe's meadow, where it unites with the brook above named. The third takes its rise in the southwesterly portion of the town, and joins the above brook just over the Spencer line. These three forks are the head-waters of the Chicopee River, that rising on the Partridge land being the most easterly, and, perhaps, is the true head of the Chicopee.

The head-waters of the Blackstone River are found on the old Col. Snow Farm, and near the road leading from Paxton to Holden. The spring is on land now owned by Peter Daw. There are numerous other springs lower down the brook which is known as Arnold's Brook. The stream was given the last name of Oliver Arnold, who lived in the present old red house, adjoining the highway at the junction of the Worcester and Leicester roads; he kept a saw- and grist-mill there, and had an artificial reservoir, which has since been enlarged and repaired, and, like the brook flowing into it, was and is called Arnold's Pond. The old saw-mill site is still visible, a few rods west of the county road. Mr. Arnold had a son Elisha, who is living in this town at the present time. The pond last named is used as a storage reservoir for the mills below, and its waters flow into Bottomly Pond, previously mentioned.

There is another small stream, which has its source in a spring on the southeast face of Asnebumskit Mountain, and flows across the county road southerly, and is the head-water of Lynde Brook which forms a source of supply for the city of Worcester.

While speaking of these brooks, we are reminded of a house in this town, owned and occupied by Tyler S. Penniman, situated about a mile east of the village. This house stands on a slight rise of ground, in such a way that rain falling upon the roof flows away into the waters of the Blackstone River on the one side, while upon the other the water goes to the Chicopee. There is, too, a well-known spring, famed for its cool, sweet water, which bubbles up near the trunk of a large tree just west of the Rutland highway, and less than a mile from the centre, where the water flows a short distance into a marshy tract, out of which two streams come, one going northerly into the Quinepoxet, while the other goes southerly to the Chicopee.

The original growth of forest trees here must have been quite large and very general. At the present time pine and hemlock predominate, though there are samples of about every other sort of timber found in New England. As an illustration of the size of some of the earlier timber, it may be interesting to note that this sketch is penned on a table made of a single pine board, three and a half feet in width, manufactured from a tree cut in this town some fifty years ago. The older growth of wood disappeared long since, and at the present time the second growth has about all been removed, and yet it would be difficult to say whether there is, or is not, as much land given up to the growth of forest trees as at any time within the past hundred or more years.

Among the early settlers in what is now Paxton, the names of Josiah Livermore and his brother, Jason Livermore, appear. This was about 1748. They came from the town of Weston, and settled in what is now the southwestern part of this town, on lands considerably improved. About the same time came Abijah Bemis, and from the same town, or Waltham. There were also living near the Livermores: William Thompson, James Thompson, James Bemis, William Wicker, Jacob Wicker, John Wicker, Isaac and Ezekiel Bellows.

Captain Ralph Earle, an early settler, owned and lived on the farm which once belonged to the late Joseph Penniman; and his was one of the first fifty families which settled in Leicester, and he was one of the grantees named in the deed of the proprietors of Leicester, and was assigned to Lot No. 47. On the other hand, in the Rutland portion of the new town, Seth Metcalf made an early settlement, as did Phineas Moore, who lived on the Rutland road, a mile or so north of the present meeting-house, and, by the way, it is proper to say that the line dividing the towns of Leicester and Rutland ran east and west, by the

2

present north side of the meeting-house as it now stands. Others of the early settlers were: John Snow, David Davis, Benjamin Sweetser, Samuel Moore, Jonathan Witt and Oliver Witt.

We have seen that the act of incorporation of the "District of Paxton" transpired on the 12th of February, 1765. Very speedily "a warrant," dated the 25th of February, 1765, was issued by John Murray, of Rutland, a justice of the peace, the same being addressed to Phineas Moore, "one of the principal inhabitants" residing within the new district, requiring him to warn a meeting of the inhabitants for the choice of officers. We append a copy of the first warrant calling the first district meeting:

Worcester ss. To Mr. Phineas Moore of Paxton in the county of Worcester and one of the principal Inhabitants of Said District. Greeting—Whereas I the subscriber am Impowered by an act of this Province to call a meeting of the Inhabitants of the District of Paxton to Choose Town Officers &c.

[SEAL] These are therefore on his Majestys name to Require you forthwith to Warn and Notify the Said Inhabitants of Paxton Qualified to Vote in Town Affairs to meet at the House of Mr. Jn°. Snows Innholder in Said Paxton on Monday the Eleventh Day of March Next at nine of the Clock in the forenoon then and there to Choose a Moderater, District Clerk, Selectmen, assessor, warden, Constables, Surveyors of highways, Tythingmen, Fenceviewers, Sealers of Leather, Sealers of weights and measures, Sealers of Boards, and Shingles, and all other ordinary Town Officers as Towns Choose in the month of March annually; hereof Fail not and make Due Return hereof with your Doings hereon unto me at or before the Said meeting. Given under my hand and Seal at Rutland in Said County this 25th Day of Feb. 1765 and in the fifth year of his Majesty's Reign.

JNO. MURRAY, Jus. of the Peace.

This first town-meeting was at the house of one John Snow, who kept a tavern or hotel, and who lived just east of the present village, on the Holden road, on the place known to the present inhabitants of Paxton as the old Colonel Snow or Bellows place. This place has now no farm buildings upon it, they having been destroyed by an incendiary fire about ten years since.

The meeting was held on March 11, 1765. Captain Samuel Brown was chosen moderator, and Ephraim Moore district clerk, and the following district officers elected, namely: Selectmen, Oliver Witt, Ephraim Moore, Samuel Brown, Timothy Barrett, Abraham Smith; Clerk, Ephraim Moore; Treasurer, Ephraim Moore; Wardens, William Thompson, Jr., Jonathan Knight; Assessors, Oliver Witt, Ephraim Moore, Aaron Hunt; Constable, John Livermore; Surveyors of Highways, Abner Moore, Ebenezer Hunt, Jr., Elijah Howe, Thomas Cutler; Sealer of Weights, etc., Captain Samuel Brown; Tything-men, Samuel Man, Ralph Earle; Hog-reeves, Jonathan Morse, William Martin; Deer-reeves, James Ames, William Whitaker; Pound-keeper, Jonathan Knight; together with other officers, such as measurers of boards and shingles, etc.

They probably had a jollification at the close of this meeting. Remembering that in those early days the inhabitants had no town halls, either old or new, in which to meet, their next best place was at some public house, or tavern, as they were then called, and we have seen that they first gathered at an inn. In those they found good cheer, even if the accommodations were circumscribed. Here, too, the old-time flip-mug, or glass, served for the whole company, and was frequently replenished, as everybody in those days indulged, more or less, in the "flowing bowl." It is sometimes asserted in these days that temperance has not made any progress, but in these century mile-stones we can note a world of advancement. Why, a hundred years ago the clergy, as well as the people, partook of the ardent, even at the laying of the corner-stones and dedication of church edifices, and also after the Sabbath sermon all would repair to the nearest tavern for "refreshment." Now, in New England these things have all passed away, so far as the public eye or public approval is concerned. Strange to say, however, the people did not lack for piety in those sturdy days, for among the very first things done, of note, by this district of Paxton was to provide by vote for the building of a "meetinghouse."

At the next district meeting, held on April 1, 1765, "it was put to vote to see if the district will Build a Meeting House in said Paxton and of what dimensions they will Build it, also to see if the district will agree upon some place for to Sett Said meeting House on." It was also voted "to build a house of worship fifty feet in length and forty in width with twenty two foot posts and to set the house at the Gate behind John Snow's farm in Mr. Maynard's pasture."[1] In the following autumn a grant was made of £13 6s. 8d. for the support of the gospel during the winter. In

---

[1] During the year a good deal of dissatisfaction was manifested about the location, and several efforts were made, at subsequent meetings, to change the decision, and we believe it was finally located on land of Seth Snow, who subsequently gave the town the land around it for a town "common."

the following spring (March 3, 1766), the sum of £250 was voted " for a meeting house and a meeting house place." When the building had advanced to the point of raising the frame there was a general turn-out of the citizens interested, and the records say a supper was provided for the occasion. The building was so far completed by the end of the year that its use commenced. Its appearance has been described by Mr. Livermore,[1] in his Centennial address, as " a plain, square structure, standing in the middle of the Common in primitive simplicity, without dome or spire, destitute of external ornament and internal embellishments, its prominent sounding-board above, and its deacon seat and its semi-circular communion table at the base of the pulpit; its uncarpeted aisles and pen-like pews, with their uncushioned and hinged seats, to be turned up and let down at the rising and sitting of their occupants, with a clatter sufficient to have awakened a Rip Van Winkle; its negro seats in the rear of the front gallery and the old people's in front of the pulpit, for the use of the deaf; its two corner pews perched aloft over the gallery stairs.

" ' Through which, and the scuttles above, were the ways
To the attic, the arsenal of those early days.' "

Thus did the inhabitants of this new district of Paxton keep faith with the General Court. They had asked to be set up in housekeeping, and gave as a reason that it was burdensome and extremely in-convenient for them to go so many miles to attend

---

[1] George W. Livermore, of Cambridge, a native of Paxton, delivered the Centennial address in 1865.

upon church service, and it cannot be denied that they were sincere and honest in their request. They had, indeed, other and important reasons for separation, but the foregoing was the chief one given.

One writer says that there was an attempt to form at first an Episcopal Church, but it failed, and had the effect to put off the formation of any other till September 3, 1767, when the present Congregational Church was organized, and the meeting-house completed during this year.

Regular preaching heretofore had not been established, but yet services had been held by the Rev. Henry Carver and by Rev. Mr. Steward, who also taught school here at this early date in the history of Paxton.

The names of those subscribing to the covenant at the time of organization were Phineas Moore, John Snow, Jason Livermore, David Davis, Benjamin Sweetser, Silas Bigelow, Samuel Man, Oliver Witt, Stephen Barrett and Samuel Brown.

In the early part of 1767 a committee was appointed to secure a permanent pastor, and they subsequently reported in favor of the Rev. Silas Bigelow. On May 14, 1767, the district voted him the sum of £133 6s. 8d., as a settlement grant, and also voted a yearly salary of £53 6s. 8d. for the first four years, and £66 13s. 4d. as long as he shall continue his relations as a minister.

In response to the call of the parish and district of Paxton to become their settled pastor, the Rev. Silas Bigelow returned the following answer, viz.:

To ye Inhabitants of ye District of Paxton, Christian Friends and Brethren:

I have taken very serious Notice of ye Sovereign Hand of Divine Providence in Conducting me to you, and would in some suitable and Grateful manner attend to ye kind acceptance my labours have met with among you ; and ye Regard which you have manifested to me (how unworthy so ever) in Electing me to be your Pastor. I observe ye Degree of unanimity and undeserved Affection with which you have Done this, and I can't but be apprehensive of *Harmony* and *unanimity* afford some of ye Best encouragements to hope for success, and yt ye Great End of ye Gospel ministry may be obtained in the Conversion of Souls to God and ye edifying of Saints in Faith and Comfort to Salvation. Nor would I fail to take Due Notice also of ye Provision which you Have made for my *Settlement* and *Support* among you ; and it is Fit you should give Praise to God who both enabled you to maintain ye gospel and ye ordinances thereof, and so far inclined your hearts thereto ; At ye same time I am obliged to appraise you (not, I hope, From any avoricious Disposition, nor Because I would rather seek yours than you, but because I would fain Promote your real Benefit and highest welfare) that after Taking ye Best Advice I can get, not merely From those in Ministerial life, but From others in Civil Character, I fear I shall not be able (from The *Support* you have *offered*) to answer your expectations from me in ye office I must Bear, nor to sustain the Dignity and Discharge the duties thereof. But having sought earnestly to ye God of all Wisdom and Grace for Direction in the most weighty and important affair ; Consulted such as are esteemed Respectable for their Capacity and Integrity, and Deliberately considered everything as well as I could within myself, I accept of your Call, Determining by the Grace of God to Devote myself to ye work of ye Gospel Ministry among you ; not Doubting your Readiness to Do what you can to free me from ye unnecessary cares and Incumbrances of Life ; yt so I may more fully give up myself to this Great and arduous work. Concluding with Rom. 15: 30 and 32. Now I Beseech you, Brethren ; for ye Lord Jesus' sake and for ye love of ye spirit yt ye strive together with me in your prayers to God for me ; That I may come unto you with Joy by ye will of God, and may with you be refreshed. So Prays your Friend and Servant in the Gospel of Christ.

Paxton, June 25, 1767.   SILAS BIGELOW.

Mr. Bigelow was ordained on October 21, 1767. His pastoral labors were comparatively of brief duration, since his decease occurred on November 16, 1769, at the age of thirty years. He was buried in the public cemetery, near the southeast corner and but a few paces from the present meetinghouse. All accounts agree that this first pastor was a devoted minister of the Gospel; a man of unusual intellectual endowments, coupled with great dignity of manner, and he was also a man much esteemed for his high Christian character and greatly beloved by all of the parish over which he had so briefly presided.[1]

Under his ministry the kindliest of feeling had sprung up among all the members of the society, and had his valuable life been spared to this people, much greater good must have been accomplished. The Rev. Mr. Bigelow was from the vicinity of Concord, it is believed; of his early education we have no present data. He was of a family, however, quite celebrated for their learning and prominence in public affairs.

He lived on the western slope of Asnebumskit, on what is now known, and has been these many

---

[1] The undersigned met on Nov. 9, 1767, and made choice of pews in the completed church. The prices they were to pay ranged from fourteen to twenty-two dollars. The district voted to give them the preference as to choice, since they were the heaviest tax-payers on real estate. The district also voted to give them deeds of the pews.

Capt. Oliver Witt, Timothy Barrett, Abraham Smith, Capt. Ephraim Moore, Hezekiah Newton, Capt. Samuel Brown, Jonathan Smith, Elijah How, Jeremiah Newton, Jonathan Knight, Samuel Man, Ebenezer Hunt, Jr., James McKennen, Capt. Ralph Earle, Paul How, Phineas Moore, Jacob Sweeter, Ebenezer Hunt, Abijah Bemis, Peter Moore, Abner Morse, David Davis, William Whitaker, William Thompson, Seth Snow.

years, as the "old Bigelow place." His first wife was from Lexington. There is one memento of this family still preserved. It is an antique clock, one of the well-known "grandfather's clocks," so-called, reaching from floor to ceiling. It was a bridal present from her parents in Lexington, where the clock was made, as indicated on its face. It remained in the family several generations and on the farm more than one hundred years, and is now in the possession of the wife of the writer (a descendant), and is doing duty as faithfully as when first set in motion by the hand of the bride, a century and more since. His second wife was a Mrs. Sarah Hall, of Sutton; intentions of the marriage were published September 22, 1769, as shown by the records.

On November 28, 1770, the Rev. Alexander Thayer[1] was ordained as the successor of Rev. Silas Bigelow. His pastorate continued for nearly twelve years. He was dismissed on August 14, 1782. His relations with the church during the last half of his ministry were anything but agreeable. He was suspected of being a loyalist. "This suspicion (says one writer), whether well or ill-founded, was sufficient to create a degree of coldness, and, in some instances, a fixed dislike, especially among those, who, from other causes, had become disaffected." It is reported that his salary was another cause of trouble, he complaining that the currency had much depreciated, and that he was justly entitled to a grant to make it equivalent to what it was when first settled, and it is not un-

---

[1] He married Miss Abigal Goulding, of Holliston, in 1773.

likely, from a review of the whole matter, there was really just ground for complaint upon both sides, and entire condemnation of either party would be very unjust.

The Rev. John Foster[1] followed Mr. Thayer. He found the church divided and inharmonious. He endeavored to reconcile them, but was unfortunate in being a positive man, and in expressions was perhaps injudicious.

At all events the old troubles were not healed, but broke out afresh, when it was proposed to settle him. The first council refused to grant a settlement, but a short time afterwards a new council, composed of different members from the first, voted to ordain and settle him, which was accordingly done on September 8, 1785. He was dismissed in 1789. During his pastorate there was a secession of about twenty, who formed a new church, and so continued till 1793, when a reunion occurred.

Mr. Livermore relates several anecdotes of Mr. Foster, one of which will interest the general reader. "In those days, when capital punishment was to be inflicted it was the law that public religious exercises should be held, and the criminal had the privilege of selecting the preacher. Mr. Foster was selected, and at the appointed hour the house was crowded, and in the audience were many clergymen. Mr. Foster being selected only to preach, asked the first minister he saw to offer prayer. The invitation was declined, and

---

[1] He was married in September, 1785, to Mrs. Eunice Stearns, of Holden.

several others were similarly invited and all declined, whereupon Mr. Foster stepped to his place, with the remark in an undertone, though loud enough in the general hush of the occasion to be heard by all, 'Thank God, I can pray as well as preach.' It is reported that his prayer was so soul-stirring and sincere that all were moved to tears, and many wept aloud."

Mr. Foster is reported to have been a man of brilliant attainments, and a very eloquent preacher, but possessed some other qualities that neutralized greatly these gifts. The Rev. Daniel Grosvenor was installed on the 5th November, 1794, as the successor of Mr. Foster. He came to this people from a church in Grafton, where he had been pastor. There was, for a season, quiet and considerable religious interest manifested under this affable and able pastor. But the old trouble would not wholly down, but, ghost-like, came to the surface.

Mr. Grosvenor's health was poor at best, and he felt unequal to the task of reconciling the factions, and finally asked to be dismissed, which was granted on November 17, 1802.

One proof that the old troubles were the causes of the unhappy condition of things at the time, and prior to the retirement of Mr. Grosvenor, is that they continued to be a disturbed church for several years after he left, and some years came and went before a pastor was again settled over them.

Mr. Grosvenor lived a half mile northeast of the church on the Holden road, where Peter Daw now lives.

In 1808, February 17th, the Rev. Gaius Conant was ordained, and he remained with the society for many years. He lived and died in the square-roofed house now occupied by Deacon Levi Smith, situated about half a mile due east from the church. He was dismissed September 21, 1831, and the same council ordained the Rev. Moses Winch. It was in 1830 that the Congregational Society was organized separately from the town. Mr. Winch's ministry must have been a very quiet one, and without any very disturbing circumstances, since very little is said respecting his stay here. He was discharged in 1834, August 28th.

The Rev. James D. Farnsworth succeeded Mr. Winch and was ordained on the 30th of April, 1835, and continued his labors till May 7, A.D. 1840. He was succeeded by the Rev. William Phipps, A.M., who was ordained November 11, A. D. 1840. Something more than a passing notice should be given this eminently gifted divine. He was for more than twenty-eight years connected with the history of the Congregational Church in this town. He was born in Franklin, this State, on October 31, 1812. He was the son of William and Fannie (Moulton) Phipps, with a line of ancestry traceable back to old England; to the father of Sir William Phipps, one of the early Governors of Massachusetts Colony. He was a quiet, gentle man, and true, yet did not lack force or bravery. He was resolute for worthy ends, and brave in self-denial. He early learned the trade of a cabinet-maker in his father's shop, which trade, in those days, meant quite as much an ability to manufacture a violin as a bureau, and as an illustration of his mechanical genius in this direction, it is told that he made in the days of his apprenticeship a fine bass-viol, with five strings, on which he was wont to play as an accompaniment to his vocal songs. He was a great lover of music and possessed a fine, rich, bass-tone voice, and always sang with an enthusiasm never to be forgotten by sympathetic hearers. He found his trade especially useful to a "country minister" in a small place, and on a small salary, since many of the things he needed he either had to make or go without. His inventive faculty was by no means inconsiderable. He constructed models of an improved school-room, a turret wind-mill, a drawing globe, a seed-sower, an upright piano and other useful and fancy things. He was a natural student, ever fond of the companionship of good books, and was diligent in everything. He attended Day's Academy in Wrentham; from there he entered Amherst, and graduated in the class of 1837. On leaving college he taught, as principal, in the academy at Edgartown, for one year. He married, in 1837, Miss Mary C. Partridge, of Franklin, who still survives at the age of eighty-eight. They had seven children, of whom five are living—two sons and three daughters. The sons, George G. and William H., have taken up the profession of their father. The former is settled at Newton Highlands, while the latter is preaching in Prospect, Conn. Mr. Phipps was first settled in this town. He was an earnest preacher and profoundly interested in all good works. He served for very many years as the head of the School Committee, and his school reports are good reading to-day, and display much thought, earnestly and gracefully expressed. He was wont to do anything he had in hand with "all his might," whether tuning a piano, or raising the finest vegetable in town. Those, whether in the church or out who became intimate, were not the ones to turn from him, for they best realized his largeness of heart and generosity of spirit.

But few of his sermons were ever published, barring a few Thankgiving discourses, fugitive pieces in various newspapers and a number of musical compositions.

Of the latter, it was as easy for him to write the poetical stanzas as the melodies that floated them. Had he been more favorably situated, as to leisure and means, he might readily have made his mark as an inventor or author, but he preferred to remain where he felt an all-wise Providence had placed him. His mark was, however, made honestly and deeply on the generation of youth that grew up under his long and faithful ministry here.

In 1869 he accepted a call to Plainfield, Conn., and was there installed June 9th. He died on June 18, 1876.

The Rev. Thomas L. Ellis succeeded Mr. Phipps, and was installed November 26, 1871. He died, after a brief pastorate, on November 12, 1873. He was followed by the Rev. Francis J. Fairbanks. He was hired in the early part of 1874, and continued his labors here till October, 1877. He was a well-educated man, and devoted in his work. The Rev. Otis Cole, a Methodist divine, was next hired by this society, and commenced his labors on January 1, 1878, and continued for two years, when he removed to New Hampshire. He was a man of great simplicity, and yet of very great power as a preacher and much beloved by all, both by those in and out of the church. The following summer the society engaged Mr. John F. Dodge, who was licensed to preach. He filled the pulpit for several years and was then ordained and settled, continuing his labors a couple of years thereafter. In June, 1887, he asked for a dismissal, having been called to the church in Sterling. Both Mr. and Mrs. Dodge were earnest in their labors in behalf of the church and community.

The Rev. Alpha Morton succeeded to the pastorate. He was engaged in June, 1887, and still continues his active labors with this people. He is an able man and of the highest character.

The old church edifice erected by the district of Paxton in 1767, paid for by a general tax, was used for all town-meetings after its erection, and the "deacon's seat" was the place occupied by the moderator of the town-meetings. In 1835 it was voted to remove the building to its present site and both enlarge and repair it, the town putting in a basement story for a town-hall, and it is now a very dignified edifice of the usual village style. Subsequently the church, feeling the need of a room for vestry purposes, entered into an agreement with the town, offering to light and warm and care for the said town hall for all town purposes on condition of its use by them as a vestry. In 1888 the town, stimulated by the gift of one Simon Allen, erected a new town hall, concerning which additional particulars are given further on in our history.

Leaving the history of the church and taking up that of the town, it will be remembered that the "District of Paxton" was chartered in 1765, Feb. 12th, and was "to join Leicester and the precinct of Spencer" in electing a Representative to the Legislature. This restriction was removed by an act bearing date July, 1775, viz.: " Whereas there are divers acts or laws heretofore made and passed by former General Courts or Assemblies of this Colony for the incorporation of towns and districts, which, against common right and in derogation of the rights granted to the inhabitants of this Colony by the charter, contain an exception of the right and privilege of choosing and sending a representative to the Great and General Court or Assembly. Be it therefore enacted and declared by the Council and House of Representatives in General Court assembled, and by the authority of the same, that henceforth every such exception contained in any act or law heretofore made and passed by any General Court or Assembly of this Colony for erecting or incorporating any town or district, shall be held and taken to be altogether null and void, and that every town and district in this Colony consisting of thirty or more freeholders and other inhabitants qualified by charter to vote in the election of a representative, shall henceforth be held and taken to have full right, power and privilege to elect and depute one or more persons being freeholders and resident in ·such town or district, to serve for and represent them in any Great and General Court or Assembly hereafter to be held and kept for this Colony according to the limitations in an act or law of the General Assembly, entitled an act for ascertaining the number and regulating the House of Representatives, any exceptions of that right and privilege contained or expressed in the respective acts or laws for the incorporation of such town or district notwithstanding."

On August 22, 1774, the following committee was chosen to consult and report on the state of public affairs, viz.: Capt. Ralph Earle, Lieut. Willard Moore, Dea. Oliver Witt, Phineas Moore and Abel Brown. They also voted to purchase a barrel of powder in addition to the stock (some two barrels) then on hand. All the able-bodied men of all ages, capable of bearing arms, were formed into two military companies, one of which was called the "Standing," and the other the "Minute Company."[1]

On the 17th of January, 1775, thirty-three men were ordered by the town to be drafted as minutemen. They chose Willard Moore to be their captain. He went with his command on April 19, 1775, to Cambridge, on receiving intelligence of the beginning of hostilities at Lexington and Concord.

The following is a copy of the agreement of the minute-men at Snow's in 1775:

We the Subscribers, Do engage for to Joyn the Minute Men of this District and to March with them Against our Common Enemys When we are called for, if so be that the Minute Companys are kept up as

---

[1] A Committee of Safety was chosen on March 20, 1775, consisting of Willard Moore, Phineas Moore, Abraham Smith, Ralph Earle and David Davis.

witness our hands: Marmaduke Earle, Jonah Newton, David Goodenow, Jr., Abijah Brown, Joseph Knight, Clark Earle, Nathan Swan, Jonah Howe, Ithamer Bigelow, John Davis, John Pike, Phineas Moore, John Flint, Ebenezer Hunt, Thomas Lamb, Oliver Earle, Jonathan White, Hezekiah Newton, Stephen Barrett, Samuel ——, Daniel Steward, Joseph Prescott.

The duties of the committee named above were various; among other matters, to observe and report to the people the action of Congress, and also the acts of the colonists and the doings of the home government, and last, but perhaps not least, to keep watch of certain suspected Tories in the district, of whom there were a number.

Captain Willard Moore, with a number of his men, soon enlisted in the Continental Army. He was promoted to the rank of major and took part with his men in the battle of Bunker Hill, where he was killed, together with several of his men. The "standing company," already named, was commanded by Captain Ralph Earle,[1] with John Snow as lieutenant, and Abel Brown as ensign. They were chosen as officers at the district-meeting on January 17, 1775, and did valiant service, and bore their share of the hardships of the long campaigns for liberty and independence.

At the town-meeting held April 6, 1775, Lieutenant Willard Moore was chosen delegate to the Provincial Congress, held in Concord, Mass., and was instructed to "use his influence in Congress that government be assumed in case that it shall prove certain that

---

[1] Capt. Ralph Earle married the widow Naomi Kinnicutt, of Providence, in 1775.

THE HISTORY OF PAXTON. 35

Great Britain intends to enforce the late acts of Parliament by the sword."

The town, at various times during the Revolutionary period, appropriated about ten thousand pounds as bounties, besides paying heavy taxes to the Provincial government amounting to many hundreds of pounds. Then, too, there were frequent purchases of beef for the use of the army, sending as high as nine thousand pounds at one time as their quota of the supplies needed by the government "at the front."

In addition to the regular companies named, there were, the records say, many volunteers going forward on their own responsibility and their own patriotic impulse to defend their imperiled country.

In the following year (1776) the records show a warrant directed to the "Constable of the *Town* of Paxton."

There is a warrant dated May 13, 1776, calling a meeting on the 23d of that month, for the purpose of choosing "a person to represent them in the Great and General Court" that year, agreeably to a precept directed "to the town" for that purpose.

On May 23, 1776, the town made choice of Abraham Smith as its first representative to the General Court, and the record shows the clerk of the meeting to have signed himself as the *town* clerk, all records prior thereto having been signed by the district clerk.

In June, 1779, there was a special call for representatives to meet in Cambridge, for the purpose of framing a State Constitution, and under this call, on August 10, 1779, Adam Maynard was chosen as the delegate. This very year it would seem by the records that Abraham Smith continued as the representative to the General Court, while Phineas Moore was the delegate to the convention held in Concord.

These were stirring times with the colonists, and besides the care of founding States was the added one of taking up arms to maintain them and establish liberty. In all of these serious affairs the new town of Paxton discharged all of her obligations with highest credit. In the earlier contests between the French and Indians this town furnished, in 1756, five men as her quota in a call for one thousand men from Worcester and Hampshire Counties. Their names were: Ezekiel Bellows, Jacob Wicker, Jason Livermore, David Wicker and John Wicker. These men were in the command of Gen. Ruggles, and saw service at Crown Point, Fort Edward and Ticonderoga.

This town is proved by all the ancient records to have been eminently patriotic in the time of the Revolution. All of the demands for men and means were met, though doubtless their efforts at times were very great. The prolongation of the war, saying nothing of the cost incurred in getting ready for the contest, was a very serious matter, but through all these trials the true patriots never flinched.

Among their first acts was an attempt on their part to rid themselves of the name of Paxton, now odious by reason of his loyalty to and influence with the enemy of the colony. They failed in their patriotic endeavor to secure a change of name, as we have seen.

The Hon. George W. Livermore, of Cambridge, a native of Paxton, relates the following incident which happened here: Jason Livermore and his three sons were plowing in the field when informed by a messenger of the incursion of the "regulars" to Lexington and Concord, and that the company of which they were members would march forthwith. The father said: "Boys, unyoke the cattle and let us be off." No sooner said than done; and they at once made ready and marched, with the household pewter dishes melted into bullets, to Cambridge, and there joined the Continental army, and on June 17, 1775, they bore a part in the great battle of Bunker Hill. The wife and mother, Mrs. Jason Livermore, was left with a lad but twelve years of age, to cultivate the farm and care for the stock. This was successfully done, and it is further stated that she made a hundred pounds of saltpetre for the army, during the summer, in addition to her other duties." Mrs. Livermore died at the extreme age of ninety-nine years and ten months. In the following year this same Jason Livermore, together with one Samuel Brewer, of Sutton, raised a company and proceeded to Charlestown, and from there were ordered to Ticonderoga and Mount Hope, where they were stationed for some time. It is fully believed that the town of Paxton must have sent more than a hundred men into the ranks of the patriot soldiers of the Revolutionary army; and history declares that few, if any, towns contributed, proportionately, more for the achievement of our independence, according to their means, than this. It is also reported that towards the close of the war " their individual and public suffering was extreme, and at times almost intolerable;" yet at no time did their courage flag or the fires of patriotism grow dim.

The qualification for voting in 1770 was the possession of sixty pounds' worth of property or an annual income of three pounds sterling. At the first State election there were twenty-four votes cast for John Hancock for Governor. The amount assessed at this time in the town on both polls and real estate was £29,400. The State tax in 1780 was as high as £5,120, old tenor.[1]

---

[1] Among the names found in the early records it is interesting to note the following, viz.:—Dr. Saml. Stearns, who married in 1773 Sarah Witt. This Dr. Stearns was the practicing physician in this town at and before the Revolution. Then there appear the names of Samuel Gould, Capt. Ralph Earle, Ephraim Moore, Marmaduke Earle, Willard Moore, Paul How, Rev. Silas Bigelow, Ithamar Bigelow, who had sons Timothy, Silas, Lewis and Ithamar; Samuel Brown, Wm. Thompson, who had sons William and James; Danl. Upham, Hezekiah Newton, John Newhall, James Earle, Oliver Earl, Wm. Livermore, John Livermore, Braddyl Livermore. Wm. Martin, Thos. Lamb, Silas, Ezekiel and Joseph Bellows, Jacob Sweetser, Saml. Sweetser and Stephen Sweetser, David Davis, Ephm. Davis, Aaron Hunt, Jonathan Ames, Seth Swan, Jabez Newhall, John Warren, Daniel Steward, M. B. Williams, Adam Maynard, Moses Maynard, David Goodenow, John Knight, Wm. Whitaker, David Wicker, Abel Brown, Danl. Knight, John Flint, Clark Earl, Nathan Sergeant, Paul. Bemis, Benj. Cutting, Dexter Earl, David Peirce, who had sons David, Gad, Aaron and Job; James Washburn, Joseph Penniman, Hezekiah Ward, Phiny Moore, Phineas Moore, Samuel Brigham, Seth Metcalf, Benj. Wilson, Dr. Thad. Brown, Dr. Saml. Forrest, Dr. Caleb Shattuck,—these were all residents and practicing physicians, between 1765 and 1800, in this town—Samuel and Ebenezer Wait, Jude Jones, Timothy Bigelow, married Anna Earl in 1797; Ithamar Bigelow, Jr., married Sophie Earle in 1801; Daniel Abbott, D. H. Grosvenor and Jonathan P. Grosvenor, Levi Boynton, Dr. Absalom Russel, Dr. Loami Harrington, was married to Delia Newton

Provision for the education of the young was made as early as 1769 in the new district. On January 9, 1769, a warrant was issued calling a meeting to consider, among other things, the division of the town into "squadrons" or school plots, as per the recommendation of a previously-appointed committee who had reported favorably. This committee (chosen in October, 1768) consisted of Captain Oliver Witt, William Whitaker, William Thompson, Willard Moore and Jonathan Knight.

There were (in 1769) five districts established, and the committee for each "school plot" were as follows: For the Northeast, Phineas Moore, Hezekiah Newton and Stephen Barrett; for the Southeast, Daniel Stewart, James Glover and Francis Eager; for the Southwest, Abner Moore, James Thompson and Jason Livermore; for the Northwest, Abraham Smith, William Whitaker and Jonah Newton; for the Middle

---

in 1806 by Nathaniel Crocker, Esq.; Taylor Goddard, Frederick Flint, Joseph Knight, Benj. Wilson, Thomas Whittemore, Wm. Howard, Henry Slade and his sons Anthony, John and Henry ; Winthrop Earle, Braddyl Livermore, Amos Ware, Elisha Ward, Ebenezer Boluton, had children, Ebenezer, Jr., born in 1770, Silas, Jeremiah, Alpheus, Phebe, Levi, Hannah, Asa and David ; Samuel Jennison, Ebenezer Estabrook, William Earle, Robert Crocker, Emory Earle, Seth Metcalf, Jr., John Pike, Francis Pike and Clark Pike, Thomas Read, Jacob Earle, Rufus Earle, Artemas Earle, Nathan Cass, Moses Gill Grosvenor, son of Rev. Daniel Grosvenor, Geo. W. Livermore, son of Braddyl Livermore, born Oct. 15, 1794 ; Thaddeus Estabrook, Ephraim Carruth, John Brigham, Joseph Day, Nathaniel Lakin, Samuel Partridge, John Partridge, Elbridge Gerry Howe, son of Jonah Howe, born Aug. 14, 1799 ; John Howe, Jonathan Chase and son, Homer Chase ; Ralph Earle Bigelow, son of Ithamar Bigelow, Jr. ; Oliver Arnold, Amasa Earle, Silas D. Harrington, Daniel Lakin, John Bellows, Sam'l Wait, Daniel Estabrook, son of Jonah Estabrook, born in 1807 ; Jacob Earle, Dr. Edward M. Wheeler.

plot, Captain Paul How, John Snow and Ralph Earle.

The following names of the heads of families living in the several school plots or divisions, together with the number given the said divisions, must be of general interest even at this date, viz. :

Northeast School Plot, No. 1.—William Allen, Capt. Saml. Brown, En. Stephen Barrett, Aaron Bennet, Samuel Estabrook, Jno. Fersenden, Zach? Gates, Aaron Hunt, Ebenezer Hunt, Samuel Man, Phineas Man, Elijah Man, Peter Moore, Ephraim Moore, Willard Moore, Hezikiah Maynard, Hezikiah Newton, Silas Newton, Benj. Pierce, Jacob Sweetser, Jacob Sweetser, Jr., Benj. Sweetser, Ebenezer Wait, Antipas How, James Ames.

Southeast School Plot, No. 2.—Capt. Jesse Brigham, Joel Brigham, En. Timothy Barrett, Thomas Denny, Wm. Earle, Jr., Antipas Earl, Francis Eager, Newhall Earl, James Glover, Zach. Gates, Wm. Howard, Jabez Newhall, Daniel Steward, Danl. Snow, Asa Stowe, Joseph Sprague, Danl. Upham, Capt. Oliver Witt, Elijah Dix, Jedediah Newton, Ebenezer Boyington, Jon't. Wheeler, Jr., Jeremiah Fay.

Southwest School Plot, No. 3.—Ezekiel Bellows, Joseph Bellows, Abijah Bemis, Jont. Brigham, Jacob Briant, John Livermore, Abner Morse, James Nicol, Seth Swan, Wm. Thompson, Wm. Thompson, Jr., Wm. Wicker, David Wicker, Samuel Wicker, Jacob Wicker, David Newton, Jonathan Knight, Jr., James Pike, Solomon Newton.

Northwest School Plot, No. 4 (now West School District).—Joel Brigham, Jonathan Clemmer, David Goodenow, Ebenezer Hunt, Jr., James McKennon, Seth Metcalf, Jaasaniah Newton, Jonah Newton, Nahum Newton, John Smith, Abraham Smith, Jonas Smith, Wm. Whitaker, Wm. Whitaker, Jr.

The Middle School Plot, No. 5.[1] (now the Centre School).—Abel Brown. Col. Gardner Chandler, Capt. Thos. Davis, David Davis, Wm. Earle, Capt. Ralph Earle, Samuel Gould, Wid. Damarius How, Wm. Martin, Shadariah Newel, Ebenezer Prescott, David Pierce, Jonathan Knight, Daniel Knight, Jno. Snow, Seth Snow, Adam Maynard, Elijah Demmon, Capt. Paul How, Jonah How, Saml. Brewer, Eleazer Ward, James Logan, Andrew Martin.

The Northwest (or West, as it is now known) School-

---

[1] The number of districts now is the same as in 1769.

house was located, in these early days, just west of the road leading from "Hows Hill," now "Davis's Hill," to Jennison's Mills (Comins' Mills), a few rods southward of the pond and across the highway. About 1820 the present brick school-house was erected just west of the mill-dam. Some fifty years ago or more Homer Chase taught this school, and lived at the house near by. It will be recollected by the older citizens that years ago the seats were arranged in two rows, which brought the scholars in two lines, one directly back of the other.

A class in reading was up, and a notably dull scholar was proceeding, and, as usual, was being prompted by his neighbor behind him, who could overlook his book. It was the habit of this dull reader to use his finger to keep his place, and as he was being coached, his finger prevented the party prompting from seeing the words ahead, so he whispered to this dull reader, "Skip it;" the reader supposed they were the next words in order for him to repeat, and he drawled out, "S-k-i-p i-t," which had the result to "bring down the house," as modern people speak.

At the Southwest School, forty years ago, there were as many as sixty scholars in attendance, and this was true of most of the other schools in town, whereas, at the present time, they would not average a dozen pupils to a school-house, outside of the Centre District; and what is true of this town is nearly true of all the back towns in New England. The Centre School building used to stand north of its present location, near where Hiram P. Bemis now lives, on the Rutland road. It was a square-built house, and when abandoned, it was used to erect the house now owned by H. C. Eames, on the Barre road. Mr. D. Gates Davis remembers when more than sixty scholars attended at this school.

We herewith append a list of prices established in 1777 by the authorities of Paxton:

Agreeably to late act of the Great and General Court of Massachusetts Bay To Prevent Monopoly and oppresion; The Selectmen and Committee of correspondence for the Town of Paxton have Agreed upon and affixed the Prices hereafter set down to the Following Articles in the Town of Paxton, Viz. :—
Men's Labour at Farming Work in the months of July and August, 3 shill. per day; The months of May, June and September, 2s. 3d. per day; The months of April and October, 1s. 9d. per day; The months of November, December, Jan., February and March, 1s. 4d. per day; Wheat, 6s. per Bushel; Rye, 4s. 3d. per Bushel; Indian Corn, 3s.; Oats, 1s. 8d. per Bushel; Barley, 3s. 6d. per Bushel; Spanish Potatoes, 1s. per Bushel in the fall of the year and not to exceed 1s. 4d. at any other season; Beans, 6s. per bushel; Peas, 7s. per bushel; Sheeps Wool, 2s. per lb.; Fresh Pork, well fatted, 3 pence 3 farth. per lb.; Good Grass-fed Beef, 2 pence 3 farth. per lb.; Stall-fed Beef, 3 pence 3 farthing per lb.; Raw Hides, 3 pence per lb.; Green Calf Skins, 6 pence per lb.; Imported Salt, 13 shillings per bushel; Salt manufactured of Sea water, 15s. per bushel; West India Rum, 8s, 2d. per Gallon; New England Rum, 5s. per Gall.; Best Moscorado Sugar, £3 6s. 8d. per Hundred Wt. and 8 pence 3 farthings by the single pound; Molasses, 4s. 8d. per Gallon; Chocolate, 1s. 9d. per lb.; Best new milk Cheese, 5 pence 1 farthing per lb.; Butter, 9 pence per lb.; Tan[d] Leather, 1s. 3d. per lb.; Curried leather, in Proportion; Homespun yard-wide Cotton . . .; Cloth, 3s. 6d. per yard; Mutton, Lamb and Veal, 3 pence per lb.; wheat Flour, 18s. per hundred Wt.; Best English Hay, 2s. 8d. per Hundred Wt.; Teaming work, 1s. 6d. per mile for a Ton; Turkies, Dunghill Fowls and ducks, 4 pence per lb.; Geese, 3 pence per lb.; Milk, 1 penny 3 farthing per quart; Good Merchantable white pine Barn boards, 2s. 8d. per hundred feet; Men's best yarn Stockings 5s. 4d. per pair; Men's best Shoes made of neat Leather, 8s. per pair; Women's best Calf Skin shoes, 6s. 8d. per pair; Making Men's Shoes, 2s. 8d.; Making Women's leather shoes, 2s. 8d.; Good Salt Pork, 8 pence

per lb.; Cotton, 3s. 8d. per lb.; Good well-dressed merchantable Flax, 1 shilling per lb.; Coffee, 1s. 5d. per lb.; Yard wide tow Cloth, 2 shillings per yard; Good yard-wide Stripped Flannel, 3s. per yard; Fried Tallow, 7 pence per lb.; Rough Tallow, 4 pence 2 farth. per lb.; Men's board, 5s. per week; Women's board, 2s. 8d. per week—. Taverners; Oats, 2 pence 2 farthings for 2 Quarts; A mug of Flip made with half a pint of West India Rum, 1s. 1d.; a mug of Flip made with half a pint of New England Rum, 9 pence; a Common meal of Vituals, 9 pence; lodging a person a night, 4 pence; Keeping a horse a night or 24 hours on English Hay, 1 shilling; Keeping a yoke of oxen a night or 24 hours on English Hay, 1 shilling; Charcoal, 3 pence per bushel at the pit; Shoeing a horse round and Steeling toe and heel, 6s. 3d.; Weaving Plain Towel Cloth yard-wide, not to exceed 3 pence 2 farthings per yard; sawing White pine boards, 1s. 1d. per Hun^d feet; Tanner's Bark Oak—Delivered at the Yard, 12s. per Cord—price for tanning, 1 penny 3 farthings per lb.; horse hire, 2 pence per mile; Cyder not to exceed 6s. at the press in time of the Greatest Scarcity; Carpenter's work, 3 shilling per day; Price of Taylor's work to be advanced one-eighth part above what was usual when Labour at farming work in the Summer Season was 2s. 8d. per day; Best Homespun Woolen Cloth of a Good Colour full^d and Press^d not to exceed 8s. per yard, and all other articles not her enumerated are to bear a price in a just Proportion to the Particularly Mentioned, According to former Customs and usages. Dated at Paxton, Feby. 7, 1777. Agreed to by the Selectmen and Committee of Correspondence of Paxton. Attest,

ABEL BROWN.

On September 14, 1791, Seth Snow, of Paxton, gave by deed to the town, one and a half acres and fifteen rods, "whereon the meeting-house stands," the whole forming nearly a square tract for "the use and benefit of the town." The bounds are given in Book 115, page 134, as certified to by Artemas Ward, register of deeds, Worcester, and are as follows, viz.:

A certain tract or parcel of common land lying in Paxton aforesaid, whereon the meeting-house stands, for the use and benefit of the said town, and is bounded as follows, viz.: beginning at a stake and stones on the south line of the burying-yard, thence East 3° S. nine rods and nine-tenths to a stake and stone, being the Northwest corner of Frederick Hunt's land; thence South 13° 40′ W. eighteen rods and eight-tenths of a rod to a heap of stones on the West side of said Hunt's barn, said line strikes the Northwest corner of said barn ; thence South 29° East ten rods and seven-tenths to a stake and stones ; thence West 12° 30″ N. four rods to a stake and stones by the Southeast corner of Deacon Timothy Barrett's horse-shed ; thence N. 32° West seven rods to a stake and stones near the Northeast corner of the store ; thence W. 8° 45′ N. eight rods and six-tenths to a stake and stones by the Northwest corner of my dwelling-house ; thence S. 45° 30′ W. six rods to a stake and stones ; thence W. 19° N. two rods and five-tenths to a stake and stones ; thence East 42° N. nine rods to a stake and stones near the Southeast corner of Abner Morse's horse-stable ; thence N. 8° E. running on the West side of the horse-stables eighteen rods to the first-mentioned corner; said tract contains one acre and a half and fifteen rods by measure.

The town, after about 1800, moved along the even tenor of its way, without alarming incidents, until 1812, when, at a special meeting of the town, held August 10th, of that year, it was voted to choose a committee to attend a county convention called to consider the state of the country, and Nathaniel Crocker and Braddyl Livermore were appointed as the delegates. There was also a petition or memorial ordered at this meeting to be sent to the President, and the following persons were appointed to prepare the same, viz. :—Nathan Swan, Nathaniel Lakin, David Davis, Jr., Braddyl Livermore and Jonathan P. Grosvenor. The war was of short duration, terminating in a successful issue for the government.

Of Indian history little is known. Paxton was for many years a part of other towns, and their history would in part be its history, but long before the surrounding towns were incorporated there were conflicts with the aborigines in this vicinity, though yet not much that can be localized as having happened within the present territory of the town. Yet there was one Indian resident of this town who made it his home during the greater portion of his life, and his name was Aaron Occum.[1] He was the last remnant and representative of his race. He lived about one hundred years ago, and had his home near the southwest point of Turkey Hill Pond. He lived in peace and quiet with his white neighbors, who learned to like him, and were, at times, much interested in him: "He was a tall, well-formed man, very lithe and strong, and in feats of running, jumping, wrestling or lifting, no white man in the town could approach him. He clung to his ancient arms, and always was seen with bow and arrows, and with these primitive weapons his aim was unerring and fatal. He was a temperate and peaceful man and came to be respected and was a frequent visitor during the long winter evenings, at the dwellings of his neighbors, whom, in broken English, he would entertain by his wonderful stories of his ancestors and their exploits. Close by his cabin was a large flat rock, on which he pursued his occupation of beating brooms and making baskets, in which arts he was a master, and his wares found ready sale in the vicinity. Thus he lived till one eventful winter night, when he went to visit at the old red house on the hill, a half-mile or so west of his cabin, now the home of Oris Howe. It was an icy time, bitter cold having followed a storm of sleet. The face of the country was glass, with ice. Occum finally departed, and with a bound he started forward down the hill, but he never reached his cabin

---

[1] Related to us by George Maynard of Worcester.

home alive. The next morning he was found dead at the foot of a sharp declivity, with a gash in the back of his head caused by a sudden fall on a sharp stone above the ice. He, in the darkness, had, doubtless, miscalculated his footing and thus came to his sudden death. He was buried in the public cemetery of the town."

Of Indian relics there are few; still, some are found of course, but not in numbers that would lead us to think any tribe made its permanent home on these hills. There is, however, just west of the Barre road, beyond the causeway, adjacent to the house of the late Benjamin Maynard, "a low, hollow rock," which tradition says was an Indian "Mortar," used by them for grinding corn. The story of the "Indian Graves" was related by John Metcalf, who lived to be ninety years old and had a clear memory up to the close of his long life. He died about 1884. His statement was that southwest of said Turkey Hill Pond, on a long ridge, is the spot where a party of Indians killed a number of white men, as described in a book giving an account of the Indian Wars. Here seven white men were killed and were buried under a large oak tree. The mound may still be seen surrounded (or was) by flat stones, not far from the stump of a large oak tree. The original account stated "that a party of white men were attacked on a hill at the southwest corner of a pond with a large hill on the east side of it, about ten miles from Quinsigamond (Worcester) and on the road from Quabog (Brookfield) to Wachusett, and were buried under a large oak tree." Mr. Metcalf showed this account to one

Artemas Howe, of this town, and together they identified this place as the spot referred to.

George Maynard states that at one time he sank a shaft into this mound and below yellow earth he came to a black mound, such as might appear in any very ancient grave.

Of murders there have been several within the present limits of the town since its first settlement. The first great crime of this character occurred on what is known as the old "Carruth Road," which formerly led from just below "Comins Mill" (once "Jennison's Mill") to the north into the Barre Road and on to West Rutland. Less than a half-mile from the mills named lived Daniel Campbell, a Scotchman, who was killed March 8, 1744, by one Edward Fitzpatrick, an Irishman who was in the employ of Campbell. Fitzpatrick disposed of the body in the wood-pile, the whole covered over with a few rails. There was a general rally of the neighbors to search for the missing man. It was agreed that should the body be found the horn (conch-shell) should be blown to give notice. At the sound of the horn Fitzpatrick, who was standing in the doorway of the house, exclaimed, "My God! it is all up with me," or words to that effect. Fitzpatrick was tried the following September, found guilty and sentenced to be hanged on the 18th of October following. Campbell was buried in the old cemetery at Rutland Centre, and on his tombstone is the following inscription, viz.: "Here lies buried ye body of Mr. Daniel Campbell, born in Scotland, who came into New England A. D.

1716, and was murdered on his own farm in 1774, aged 48 years. . . . Man knoweth not his time."

This Carruth Road was much used in the days of which we write, it affording a short route to Barre and that section, to people in the vicinity of Jennison's Mills; besides, many came over this road to trade at Jennison's.

One Aaron Coggswell lived on the right as you go up this road. He is the ancestor of the present Coggswells of Leicester. Beyond Mr. Coggswell lived Ephraim Carruth and further on Daniel Campbell and others. This Mr. Carruth, for whom the road was named, came from Marlboro' along with the Hows. After the murder of his neighbor, Campbell, his family, which was quite large, became discontented and he returned to Marlboro. He was a surveyor and once surveyed the farm of David Davis, who lived at C. A. Streeter's. Mr. Carruth was not in favor with Jonah How, who lived on what is now called "Davis' Hill." This How had a pasture up on the Carruth Road where he kept his sheep in summer, and each year he lost a good lamb. At the close of the season, finding a lamb gone as usual, and happening to meet Carruth, said to him that he had got a new name for his pasture and now called it Pilfershire. After that no lambs were missed. The locality still goes by the new name among the old people of the neighborhood.

Some twenty-five years ago, at the time of grading the Great Road, as the Barre Road was then called, many men were employed, among whom was one Doyle, an Irishman. He boarded at the first house beyond the brook on what is now called the West Road (New Braintree Road), a quarter of a mile or less west of the Common. In the evening of May 11, 1862, one Henry Watson, an Englishman, was going by to his home, known as the Stillman Smith place, beyond Pudding Corner. As he came opposite the house some conversation occurred with this Doyle, who demanded some rum of Watson, which he refused, whereupon Doyle became angry, and stepping to the woodpile, took up a hemlock stick and chased Watson, who ran to the next house, where Samuel Peirce lived, and as he passed on to the veranda at the west side of the building he was struck and killed. Doyle at once fled to Worcester, where he was arrested, tried and sentenced to a long term of imprisonment at hard labor.

There was, some years ago, a human skeleton found in the front yard of a small farm-house, now occupied by H. Sweetser, on the road leading to Pine Hill, in the northerly part of the town. This brought to mind the fact that a peddler by the name of Livermore, who staid over-night in this neighborhood, some years prior, was suddenly missed from the community, and was thought to have been foully dealt with, as a quarrel was believed to have occurred at Widow Samuel Sweetser's that night. An inquest was held, but nothing was established, though Benjamin Maynard, who was present, stated that some of the parties living there were much disturbed and seemed guilty. At all events, the principals soon after left, and have never returned.

A man by the name of Charles Conners, in February, 1862, was frozen to death in his sleigh at the foot of the hill near Pudding Corner, on the New Braintree road, east of the school-house. He had been to Worcester, and, addicted to drink, had procured a bottle of liquor, and, over-indulging, had become insensible from two causes,—the liquor and the cold. The day had been somewhat mild and fairly pleasant, but in the early afternoon the wind rose and it grew cold rapidly, and before sunset the wind had risen to a blizzard, and the thermometer dropped during the night to 30° below zero. He was found in the morning, sitting nearly upright, with his hat off and an empty bottle beside him. The reins had become tangled, and had turned the horse to the side of the road, where he stopped, and was yet alive. The man lived at North Spencer, and the team belonged to Samuel Cunningham, of that place. The day he was found the thermometer at noon stood at 28° below, the coldest day for three-quarters of a century in this locality.

At one time in the spring of the year, as a company of workmen were engaged repairing the road near the present town-farm, Captain B—— was holding the plow when a skeleton was turned up. All were horror-stricken, and the captain left and went to work elsewhere, being unable to witness the scene. It was told by him that it must be the body of a Mrs. Hunt, who had lived on the cross-road near by, and who, having died of the small-pox, was hurriedly buried there. But this was not credited by the citizens. The other theory was that a young man, who, a year before, was working for the captain, had suddenly disappeared without any very good explanations, and it was believed the body was his, especially as an investigation showed the remains to be those of a male person.

Among the notable people who were born or lived in Paxton was the Livermore family. Jason Livermore was one of the early settlers, and lived in the southerly part of the town, near Pudding Corner, and had several children.

He was in the engagement at Bunker Hill, as has already been shown, and was a man of high courage and great patriotism. He was for many years a prominent citizen here. His son Braddyl also became prominent, and was well known for his capacity to transact business, and stood high among his townsmen. His son, George W. Livermore, a graduate of Harvard, and now of Cambridge, became a distinguished citizen of that place, and returned on June 14, 1865, and delivered the historical address at the centennial celebration, and to him, as well as to other writers, are we much indebted for many of the facts herewith embodied.

Few men in our early history were as distinguished as Doctor Samuel Stearns. He was a somewhat celebrated man in his day, as well as prominent as a practicing physician. He traveled much between 1778 and '85, and he made the journey from Southern Georgia to Massachusetts on horseback. He relates leaving Georgia in February, with the trees blooming, and he so timed his journey as to reach Massachusetts in early June, having a succession of blossoms for a thousand miles. He married Sarah Witt of Paxton March 7, 1773.

In 1782 he was in Europe, and continued his travels there for several years. He published a volume of his letters from England and the Continent written in 1784.[1] He speaks of meeting Minister John Adams at the Hague, and spending some time with him in driving about the country. Doctor Stearns was very fond of art, and greatly admired the painting of Rubens, as well he might. He visited the Hague in the summer of 1784 and was a guest of John Adams, the American minister, of whom he speaks in the highest praise. In speaking of the ambassador he says his livery is the same as the American uniform. He also says that in popularity and influence at that court Mr. Adams bore the palm of the diplomatic body. He adds that Mr. Adams talks but little, but what he says is direct and forceful; that America stands indebted to him principally for three important acquisitions—the defeat of Sir Joseph Yorke and securing the patronage of Holland in a critical moment, the extension of our limits and the security of our fisheries. The headquarters of the embassy was the Grand Hotel, which Mr. Adams had purchased for the permanent quarters of United States ministers. Dr. Stearns relates an incident which, but for him, the life of Mr. Adams might have been in great jeopardy, viz.:—They were driving along the banks of a canal in Delft when a child was discovered struggling

---

[1] This volume was published by Isaiah Thomas of Worcester, in 1790, entitled, "A Tour in Holland," with a preface by John Trumbull, the celebrated author of "McFingal."

for life in the waters of the canal. Mr. Adams drew off his overcoat and was about ready to leap into the water when the Doctor interfered. At this juncture, a workman close by had made the plunge and saved the drowning child.

The Earles were numerous and prominent in the town's early history and for many years afterward. Marmaduke Earle came from Leicester and settled where Nathaniel Parkhurst now lives, about a mile west of the centre, on the Barre road. He had fourteen children.

Capt. Ralph Earle, of Leicester, was the best-known of any of the Earle family. He took a part in the Revolutionary War and performed other and valuable service. One of his sons, R. E. W. Earle, became famous as an artist. He made a painting of Niagara Falls which attracted much attention, and subsequently he resided in the South, where he became an inmate of the family of General Jackson, at the "Hermitage." He painted several portraits of the general and his family. He died there in 1837, and was buried in the garden, beside the graves of Jackson and his wife. Captain Ralph was a member of important committees raised by the town at sundry times during the Revolution; was for a time chairman of the selectmen, and occasionally served as moderator. He was also captain of the Standing Company in the Revolution.

Philip Earle[1] was a public man and was engaged in the manufacture of scythes, below Jennison's Mills,

---

[1] This Philip was a son of Marmaduke Earle and succeeded to the business of one Joel Crossman.

just west of the highway. Here he had a trip-hammer and carried on quite a business. The mills above named were first owned by one Silas Newton; he lived on Brigham Hill, where one Brigham subsequently lived. Newton had a fulling mill, besides a saw and grist-mill and shingle-mill. He sold to Samuel Jennison, who is reputed to be a rough sort of a man. He kept a *wet* grocery store in the basement of his house, and it used to be a much-frequented resort. He sold to Homer Chase, his son-in-law, who continued the store business. Homer was a son of Jonathan Chase, who lived where Horace Daniels now lives.

The Davis family was likewise conspicuous, and the first Simon Davis came from Concord to Rutland, where he had a son David, who settled in Paxton, where Charles A. Streeter now lives. He had a son David, Jr., who lived at the foot of the hill, just west of his father's place. There was a tan-yard just back of this last-named house, where considerable business was done annually. At this time there was another tan-yard near Pudding Corner, on the Bellows place, where an equal amount of tanning was done. This Davis family are the ancestors of Mr. D. Gates Davis, who, until lately, lived where Jonah Howe formerly lived.

The Peirce family came here from New Hampshire, but of all the members perhaps John D. Peirce is the most conspicuous. His father was Gad Peirce, and his grandfather David Peirce. The subject of this brief sketch came to live at the Peirce homestead, in the easterly part of the town, on the farm now owned

and occupied by Horace Peirce. He lived with Job
Peirce, an uncle. He, at the age of sixteen, decided
to secure a liberal education, and, with the assistance
of the Rev. Mr. Conant, a near neighbor, he went to
Leicester Academy. He joined the church at that
place. He fitted for college, entered Brown University and graduated with Elbridge Gerry Howe, of
this place. He married in Saugerfield, New York,
studied for the ministry and settled in York State as
a Congregational minister. He subsequently went to
Michigan and preached for a time at Marshall, and at
same time kept the post-office (in a cigar-box). When
Michigan was admitted into the Union he was appointed State Superintendent of Instruction. He took
an active part thereafter in all educational affairs and
advised a liberal policy for the State, which was
adopted, and has left its impress on that great Commonwealth to this day. He was at one time prominently named for United States Senator, but being a
Whig and they in the minority, he decided to change
his politics, and soon after the party he espoused became the minority and so he died a disappointed man
in some respects. But his life was made valuable to
his fellow-men in the founding of a new State.

Of the Harringtons, first came Nathan Harrington
from Weston and settled on the farm just north and
under the shadow of Pine Hill. He had children—
Nathan, Lemuel and Samuel. The first son settled
in Barre, Vt., the second lived and died in Hardwick,
Mass., while Samuel remained at home and had
children—Lucy B., Elizabeth F., Samuel D., Lemuel,
David, Simon G., Abigail and Lucinda. Samuel D.

had children—Samuel, who lives in Boston; Nathan, living in Toledo, Ohio; and Eliza, who married Rev. Charles Morris and lives in Gloucester.

David Harrington, last above named, married Miss Olive Holmes in October, 1830. He lived and died on his farm in Paxton. He celebrated the fiftieth anniversary of his marriage on October 29, 1880. There was a large company of relatives and friends from far and near present on that occasion. Mr. Simon G. Harrington is still living at the advanced age of eighty years and upwards, at his farm on the Rutland Road. He represented the town some years since in the Legislature and is one of the brightest and ablest men in this vicinity.

Silas D., son of Dr. Loami Harrington, was a very prominent man in the public affairs of this town. On November 17, 1877, he celebrated his fiftieth wedding anniversary. He died suddenly soon after, while on a visit to Millbury. He was for many years one of the selectmen and much respected. His portrait can be seen in the new town hall.

The Howe family is a numerous one in Paxton, and the first settler here was one John How, who came from Marlboro', Mass., in 1742, and purchased lands of an agent of the Crown, and the old deed, now in possession of Dr. A. J. Howe, bears the seal of the colonial government. The place purchased by John Howe is now owned by Deacon Keep, and is situated about a mile west from the centre. This John Howe deeded the place to his son Paul Howe, and he to his son John, and he to Samuel H. Howe, the father of the present Dr. Andrew Jackson Howe, of Cincinnati. Of the Howe family born in Paxton, Dr. Howe is the most distinguished. His father moved to the edge of Leicester, where Mr. Watts now lives. At the age of twenty, Andrew bought his time of his father, agreeing to pay one hundred dollars for his "freedom," a transaction not unknown in those days. Young Howe worked in a saw-mill and thereby kept his engagement with his father as to the payment of the "time" or freedom money. He then went to Grafton, where he worked for an uncle in a shoe-factory. While thus engaged he made the acquaintance of Dr. Calvin Newton, who, being interested in him, consented to take Andrew as a student on condition that he acquire the education requisite to enter college. The young man, nothing daunted, subsequently entered the Leicester Academy, where he attended two years, taking high rank as a student, From there he went to Cambridge and was admitted, and during the four years there he held a reputable place in his class, that of 1853. While fitting for college he was obliged, out of study hours and during vacations, to labor at whatever his hands could find to do ; sometimes he was busy with wood-chopping and threshing and boat-building. After graduation at Harvard he prepared his way as best he could pecuniarily for entering upon a course of medical lectures at Jefferson College, in Philadelphia. The next year he attended hospital instructions in New York. The year following he took temporary charge of Dr. Walter Burnham's practice in Lowell, Mass. In 1855 he was appointed to the professorship of surgery in the Eclectic Medical Institute of Cincinnati, Ohio, a position he has held ever since.

He is the author of a treatise on General Surgery, and also of works on special branches of surgical science. He has, during his residence in Cincinnati, performed all the great operations of a surgical character and he is favored with a wide range of patronage. In 1886 Dr. Howe made a tour of Europe, visiting the famous hospitals of the Continent, and became acquainted with the distinguished men of his profession. As a recreative indulgence, Dr. Howe has cultivated a taste for biological investigations, and has acquired some distinction, as an anatomist. For many years he was one of the curators in the Cincinnati Society of Natural History. Dr. Howe married, in 1858, Georgiana, the oldest daughter of George Lakin, of this place.

The familiar faces of Dr. and Mrs. Howe are occasionally seen in town revisiting the places familiar in their childhood, and renewing old acquaintances, by whom they are ever cordially welcomed.

Jonah How lived on Davis Hill, and died there aged eighty-four years. Artemas How was also prominent in public affairs.

Rev. Elbridge Gerry Howe, son of Jonah Howe, was a graduate of Brown University, and went West on missionary work and established the first Congregational Church at Waukegan, Ill. He was four times married. He leaves two sons, E. G. Howe, Jr., and Ira Howe. Rev. Mr. Howe was one of those men who left the world better by having lived in it. He was pre-eminently adapted to missionary labors, in which he had great success. He was always an earnest speaker and always found on the side of right on every public question. He was an honest man and of exalted character.

The Grosvenor family were among the notable people during their residence in this town. A brief sketch has already been given of the Rev. Daniel Grosvenor. Jonathan P. Grosvenor was a prominent man, occupying offices of trust and honor for many years. He was a justice of the peace, and lived on the farm now owned by Peter Daw. Here met some of the most cultivated people in town. His daughter, Lucy Grosvenor, married David Manning, Sr., of this place, and subsequently they removed to Worcester, where they at present reside.

Capt. Tyler Goddard, who lived just north of the meeting-house at the junction of the Rutland and Holden roads, was the first postmaster in Paxton. The office was established December 10, 1816, and he held the place till 1841. He kept a small grocery store just across the road west of his house, in what is now the new burying-ground. An anecdote is related of him that one time, in order to cure David Sweetser of the bad habit of borrowing jugs, filled one for him in which oil had been kept. *This* jug came back and with it the lost jugs, and a pretty free expression of miscellaneous statements on the part of Sweetser, to the great amusement of Capt. Goddard. Luther Goddard, of Worcester, is a son of Tyler, and was for some years the town clerk of Paxton. The next postmaster was S. D. Harrington, followed by Otis Pierce, and in 1861 Nathaniel Clark was appointed and still holds the office. Of town clerks Ephraim Moore was first and William H. Clark, the present incumbent, the last chosen.

The Bigelows have ever been prominent in town since the advent of the Rev. Silas Bigelow. He had a brother, Ithamar Bigelow, who also lived on Asneybumskeit and he had sons Silas and Ithamar, Jr. Silas Bigelow had children: John Flavel, George Norman, Artemas E. and Adaline E. Ithamar Bigelow, Jr. had children: Ralph Earle, Walter R. and Lewis. Ralph Earle Bigelow had children: Caroline, Emeline and John C. Lewis Bigelow had children: Henry, Charles, Edward, George, Phœbe and Eliza.

In the late Civil War this town contributed seventy-four men, and of this number fifteen lost their lives while in the service. The records show that on the 26th July, 1862, a bounty of one hundred and ten dollars was voted. On August 9th the amount was raised eighty-five dollars. On December 8th the town offered one hundred and ten dollars for nine months' men, and one hundred and sixty dollars for those enlisting for three years. These offers were in addition to any bounties or gratuities proffered by the State or United States governments. There was an additional bounty offered in June, 1864, of one hundred and twenty-five dollars. In the year 1871 a granite monument was erected on the "Common" in memory of those losing their lives during the four years' contest with the Southern States. An iron railing surrounds this shaft, and within the inclosure there are four cannon donated by Congress. On this shaft are the names of twenty-one of our soldiers who died by reason of the Rebellion.

On June 14, 1865, the town celebrated the centennial of its incorporation. There was a large assemblage of the sons and daughters of the town on that occasion. There was a public meeting in the church, at which Hon. George W. Livermore, of Cambridge, Rev. John F. Bigelow, D.D., of Brooklyn, Prof. George N. Bigelow, also of Brooklyn, and Rev. George G. Phipps, now of Newton Highlands, delivered addresses. They were all natives of this town. A public dinner was served on the "Common," opposite the church, of which many hundreds partook. It was a grand gala occasion, and the reunions were many and most cordial, and the memory of them is as a sweet savor to all participating.

In 1888 the town erected a new town hall, in part out of the proceeds of the estate of the late Simon Allen, who left by will his entire property in trust to the town, which was to be used in the building of a town hall, the same to be called Allen Hall. The amount of his estate was twenty-two hundred dollars, but the prolonged illness of his widow reduced this amount to fifteen hundred dollars. During the lifetime of his widow the property could not be used for the purpose designated by the testator, but on her decease, which occurred in 1887, the Allen fund was turned over to the town treasurer, and at the annual meeting of the town in March, 1888, it was voted to add a thousand dollars to the Allen fund and go forward with the building, the town appointing the following persons as a building committee, viz.: L. Bill, William Brown, A. S. Graton, E. P. Keep and H. H. Pike.

The land for the location was given by the writer, and in the following July the contractor began his work, and by the 20th of the following October the building was completed, and was formally dedicated on November 1, 1888. The dedication address was delivered by Col. William B. Harding, of Worcester, the poem by George Maynard, also of Worcester, with remarks by Rev. George H. Gould, D.D., and Scripture reading and dedicatory prayer by Rev. Alpha Morton.

The chairman of the selectmen,[1] Ledyard Bill, received the keys from H. H. Pike on behalf of the building committee. The church choir, under the leadership of Oliver Goodnow, who for over fifty years has been connected with church music here, gave choice selections; the exercises in the main hall closing with America, in singing which, all joined. A public dinner was served in the lower hall by the Ladies' Union, of which Mrs. Nathaniel Clark is president. The building stands on the west side of the Barre Road, opposite the "Common." It is a plain appearing structure, but inside it is all that will be required for years to come. The total cost will not be far from forty-five hundred dollars. Simon Allen was born in 1806, in Holden, in the house near the foot of the big hill, on the Paxton and Holden Road, on the south side of the highway, and east of Mr. Metcalf's. He attended the Northeast School in

---

[1] The first board of selectmen chosen in 1765 was Oliver Witt, Ephraim Moore and Samuel Brown, while the last board chosen in 1888 was Ledyard Bill, A. S. Graton and L. T. Kirby.

Paxton a portion of his youth. He moved to Shrewsbury, where he married Miss Fannie Norcross. He was a boot and shoemaker, and followed that trade while in Shrewsbury. He moved to Paxton in 1840, and bought a farm of the elder John Slade, on the Rutland road, where George A. Brown now lives. He was a plain, unassuming, honest man, and respected by all who knew him. He died December 29, 1880, and was buried by the side of his first wife, near the west entrance to the Public Cemetery. He was twice married, but left no children.

In the year 1865, there was an agreement entered into between the town and the parish, respecting the town hall which was built by the town under the church, forming a basement story to the same. The church was removed from the "Common" to its present location in October, 1834, and repairs all completed February, 1836, and re-dedicated Feb. 24, 1836. The pews were sold by auction, and fifty-four of them brought the sum of $4,094.75. The agreement above referred to was made in 1865. It was the outgrowth of a discussion relating to the repairs which had become necessary at the time. It has always been known as the Town Hall from the commencement, and was so called both in the records of the town and parish. The repairs amounted to eleven hundred dollars. The town had previously invested six hundred dollars in this basement story to the church for a town hall, and at a meeting held March 6, 1865, under Article 16 of the Warrant, it was voted to appoint a committee of five to meet a like committee from the first parish, and, if possible, unite upon some understanding concerning the *use* of the hall and report to the town at an adjourned meeting. This they did on April 1, 1865. The committee on the part of the town, consisted of Phineas M. Howe, Otis Pierce, William Mulligan, Dwight Estabrook, and Hammond W. Hubbard. This committee submitted and recommended the following action on the part of the town, and it was—

"Voted to pay the eleven hundred dollars towards defraying the expenses recently incurred in repairing and furnishing the Town Hall, provided that in addition to the right already possessed by the town, viz: to have the right to occupy said hall for all necessary town purposes; the town shall have the right to use said hall and the rooms adjoining for all purposes allowed by the Selectmen, but in no case shall an appointment made by the Selectmen supersede an appointment made by the Parish Committee, and all moneys received for the use of said hall shall be paid to the Parish towards lighting and warming the same, provided the Parish shall have said hall insured to the amount of three-fourths of the above named eleven hundred dollars and make over the policy to the town and keep the same constantly insured. The town to be to the expense of reinsuring or renewing of said policy."

This was adopted by a vote of 32 to 10.

The above agreement was never very strictly enforced, and in the lapse of time some small discussions arose as to who possessed the right to rent the hall, and the insurance policies even run, occasionally to the Parish, and finally the Parish set up its authority to rent the hall, fix the rental, and received the funds direct from the janitor, which of course was in plain contravention of the written contract as both expressed and implied. Thus the meaning of the agreement or its interpretation frequently differed according to the prejudices of the parties in interest, and this state of affairs continued up to the time of the town's decision to go forward with the erection of a new hall under the will of Simon Allen. We would not wish to convey the impression that any serious breach was imminent, and yet it was a source of frequent irritation and probably helped somewhat in the determination of the town to accept Mr. Allen's gift and erect a separate building for its exclusive use, which was for the best interests of all concerned, except that the cost involved was much greater than was at first contemplated, or than was needful for so small a community.*

The old hall was damp and cold, and at most all times was quite unsuited for the town's use in many ways. In the new hall are quarters for the Public Library. This library was established in the spring of 1877 on the urgent representation of the writer, accompanied by a gift for its foundation, and now, after a period of more than ten years of active operation, it has proved to be an increasing educational force, and justified its establishment by the town. The present Secretary of the Trustees in control, Mr. F. Sumner Howe, in his report to the town in 1888, says :—

"From the time it was first opened till the present,

---

* The building committee received contributions to be applied to the erection of the hall from William Mulligan, Josiah Keep, C. Eugene Peirce, J. Chester Peirce, S. D. Simonds, and Charles G. Bigelow.

it has been constantly patronized by those who have sought instruction or amusement, and we believe their desires have been abundantly satisfied; not only the youth in the school room, but all ages may find in the library something to give them a greater diversity of knowledge upon a given subject, and we believe that a fair share of the intelligence and enlightenment of our people is due the library." More than thirteen hundred volumes were issued last year to its patrons.

The public schools of the town while nominally the same as a hundred years ago in point of number of districts, have in fact been reduced to four for the past few years, owing to the small number of pupils in town. The West and North-east schools are the ones which have been closed. Where fifty or sixty pupils used to attend a single school, as was the case in all of them forty years ago, there are now scarcely a baker's dozen, or even half dozen, to be found. In old times the boys and girls nearly all went to school till they were "of age," and a winter school in these rural districts was not a thing for a feminine hand to manage. It took a *master* and a pretty smart one too sometimes, to guide the helm and steer clear of rocks and shoals. Then the winter schools were crowded, and the small boy had to take his chances of getting a seat wherever one could be improvised. The school programme was not very extensive or much varied; the common English branches were thought good enough and the pupils had to be content.

Then each separate district was an independent realm in which the district committee held unlimited sway, and generally arranged to put the little kingdom of the school room, in charge of some impecunious and incompetent friend or relative, who, if he could do little else, could at least "thresh" well. There was long, determined opposition to any change, and much small talk about the invasion of the "people's rights," but the fiat of enlightened sentiment had decreed a new order of things in this regard, and the old system

> "Had to fold its tent like the Arab,
> And silently steal away."

Under the new order of things the annual appropriation by the town is usually about one thousand dollars for the support of schools. Their character here is above the average in country towns. Students have been able to enter Normal and Technical Schools and Academies from our public schools without extra training, and quite a number of fairly equipped teachers have graduated from them. Of the teachers employed years ago, two attained some celebrity, viz: Increase S. Smith and William A. Wilde—they taught at the South-west school.

Of college graduates, the following is as complete a list as it has been possible to make, viz:

Rev. MOSES G. GROSVENOR, Dartmouth,	1822
Rev. C. PITT GROSVENOR. "	1818
JOHN F. LIVERMORE, Dartmouth, . . .	1810
Prof. INCREASE S. SMITH, Brown University,	1821
Rev. ELBRIDGE G. HOWE, A. M., "	1821
Rev. JOHN D. PEIRCE, D. D., "	1822
Hon. GEO. W. LIVERMORE, LL. D. Harvard University, ...	1823
Aaron SNOW, Yale,	1835

68   THE HISTORY OF PAXTON.

Cyrus W. Conant, Union College, . 1824
Charles Livermore, Harvard University, 1825
Rev. John F. Bigelow, D. D., Brown Univ. 18—
Prof. Geo. N. Bigelow, Univ. at Berlin, 18—
Dr. Andrew J. Howe, Harvard University, 1853
Dr. Lemuel Grosvenor.
Dr. Edward R. Wheeler, Amherst, . 1860
Prof. Samuel Harrington, " . 1862
Rev. Geo. G. Phipps, . " . 1862
Rev. William H. Phipps, " . 1862
Judge Nathan Harrington, " . 1864
Prof. Josiah Keep, . " . 1874
Dr. William P. Davis, Phil. Med.
Elias W. Davis, Yale College, . . 1880
Herbert B. Howard, Harvard University, 18—
Lewellyn Harrington, Burlington Med., 1879
Wesley E. Brown, " " 1878
Edward Minturn Woodward, Amherst, 1885
Elbridge Gerry Howe, Wor. Polytechnic, 1884
Henry A. Streeter, " " 1887
Wallace Snow, Harvard, . . . 1891

He is a son of Dr. Windsor N. Snow, and a great grandson of Col. Willard Snow.

Little is known of Mr. Snow, who is reported a graduate of Yale College. Prof. Increase S. Smith taught a notable school in this town at Pudding Corner some fifty years ago. He was present at the Centennial in 1865. He has been principal of Hingham Academy and Dorchester High School.

The Rev. Elbridge G. Howe, we have already mentioned. He was born on Howe's Hill, Aug. 19, 1799. He was son of Jonah Howe, jr., and Lydia Warren. He graduated from the Andover Theological School in 1824. He was ordained a Congregational clergyman in 1824. He was settled for a time at Halifax and Marshfield in this State.

For particulars of Rev. John D. Peirce, see page 54 of this volume. We may add that in appreciation of his distinguished services to the State of Michigan, a full length portrait was secured by that commonwealth and placed, we believe, in the capitol.

The Hon. Geo. W. Livermore was a distinguished lawyer in Cambridge, and delivered the historical address at the Centennial here in 1865. His father was Esquire Braddyll Livermore, sr., son of Lieut. Jason Livermore of revolutionary fame. His ancestors were notable men and women.

The Rev. John F. Bigelow, son of Silas Bigelow, was born at the Bigelow homestead where the Henrys now live. He was a Baptist clergyman, and attained eminence as a scholar. He was settled for a time in Bristol, R. I., Middleboro', Mass., St. Albans, Vt., and in Keeseville, N. Y. He was for a few years before his decease associated with his brother at the Atheneum Seminary in Brooklyn, N. Y. He died in the latter city, June 20, 1884.

Prof. George N. Bigelow, a brother of the above, became well-known as an educator. He was for a time principal of the State Normal School at Framingham, and was principal of Atheneum Seminary above referred to. He was a ripe scholar, and in his leisure contributed various articles for educational magazines. He presided at the exercises of the Centennial Celebration here in 1865, and added much by his genial and ready wit to the success of that occasion. He was a man of fine presence, tall and portly, which was characteristic of the Bigelows of this vicinity, as we learn, for many generations.

Of Dr. Andrew J. Howe, we would refer the reader to page 56 for a biographical sketch.

Prof. Samuel and Judge Nathan Harrington are sons of Dea. Samuel D. Harrington who lived under the brow of Pine Hill in the northerly part of the town. Samuel is a teacher of the highest rank, and was at one time the head, we believe, of the Boston Latin School. Nathan is a lawyer, and lives at Toledo, Ohio, where he has acted as judge of the city court.

The Harringtons were a numerous family and occupied at one time a large section of land on the north side. At the present time only one, Dea. William H. Harrington, son of David Harrington, continues in that vicinity. He lives on his father's homestead, and also carries on a saw and box mill. These mills, we believe, were built by Dea. Morse and his son, Lewis Morse. They lived in a small one-story house a little south-west of the saw mill, which was then on the stream at the location of the present box mill. This box mill has, since we commenced this sketch, been changed to a saw mill, as in the days of the Morses. The old grist mill built by Dea. Samuel Harrington has likewise just been transformed to a box mill. The saw mill at the foot of the hill on the left of the highway is abandoned. Lewis Morse built the two-story house where Anson W. Putnam now lives, which is situated but a few rods east of the box-saw mill. The Morses sold the mills to Samuel Buttrick, who run them for at ime, when he sold to David Harrington. A short time prior to this Howard & Damon offered to lease the mills, which offer being refused, they erected the saw mill at the foot of the hill previously mentioned. They used the house of Stephen Sweetser towards the erection of the mill. This house was but a short distance away and had been abandoned by the Sweetser family.

Resuming our list of college graduates, we come to the Messrs. George G. and William H. Phipps, sons of Rev. William Phipps, a former pastor. They are both ordained Congregational clergymen and have settled pastorates, the former at Newton Highlands, while William H. is at Prospect, Ct. George G. is a scholarly man, of sparkling wit, and has something of the poet's genius.

Dr. Edward R. Wheeler, son of Dr. Edward M. Wheeler, is settled in Spencer, and succeeded to the large practice of his father. The senior Dr. Wheeler was for many years a resident and practising physician in Paxton. He married for his second wife, Miss Caroline Duncan, the sister of T. Mason Duncan. The Duncans lived where Wm. M. Warren now lives, just west of Comins's mills, now Eames's mills. The Duncans were widely known and highly respected in this community.

Prof. Josiah Keep, son of Dea. J. O. Keep, married a Miss Holman of Leicester, and settled in California, where he is engaged in teaching.

Dr. William P. Davis, son of D. Gates Davis, is a practising physician in Reading.

Elias W. Davis is engaged, at his father's homestead, in farming.

Dr. Wesley E. Brown, son of Dea. William, is living in Gilbertville.

Prof. Edward Minton Woodward, son of Albert E. and grandson of Harvey Woodward, is teaching in Worcester.

Elbridge G. Howe, son of Rev. E. G. Howe, is located in the West as a civil engineer.

Henry S. Streeter, son of Charles A. Streeter, is is engaged in teaching in this State.

The following persons have represented the town in the Legislature, viz :—Adam Smith, 1776–'84-5-7 ; Phineas Moore, 1780 ; Adam Maynard, 1781-2 ; Hezekiah Ward, 1786; Nathaniel Crocker, 1806-8-9, '13-'16; M. B. Livermore, 1810 ; Ebenezer Estabrook, 1811 ; David Davis, jr., 1814 ; Samuel Harrington, 1821 ; Tyler Goddard, 1829, '30-1-2-3-4-5-7-9 ; Artemas Howe, 1838 ; David Harrington, 1840 ; Gaius Conant, 1841-2-3 ; Samuel D. Harrington, 1849-'50 ; Simon G. Harrington, 1854 ; David G. Davis, 1856 ; Ralph E. Bigelow, 1858 ; William Mulligan, 1861-'70 ; John C. Bigelow, 1866 ; Lewis Bigelow, 1879.

The latest addition to the territory of Paxton was the northwest corner whereby the farm of Hammond Hubbard was included, also a portion of the Browning farm, thereby straightening the line and bringing within the town a fine tract of land. While the town has occasionally increased its area, the taxable valuation has for many years decreased. This has been owing to a variety of causes, chief of which has been the abandonment of boot manufacturing, and another important factor is that of fires, incendiary or otherwise. There is a neighborhood in the south-westerly side, where ten dwellings have burned down within about as many years, and all within the radius of a mile. Some of these were among the largest and best in town. Of course other parts of the town have not wholly escaped the fiery element within the time specified. The destruction of the Bigelow boot factory was a great calamity. This was situated at the south end of the village, and the firm employed many hands both in and out of the shop. The loss of the fine hotel at the centre was also greatly deplored. It was a three-story structure, and was every way a great addition to the town as well as a great convenience to the public, and was comparatively a new building. The large farm house, barn, and outbuildings on the Col. Willard Snow place, also disappeared in a few brief hours by fire. The place at the time was owned and occupied by the Bellows brothers. There are all over town many half filled cellars where former dwellings stood, and they equal in point of numbers the buildings now standing outside of the village proper.

There is still another cause operating yearly towards the reduction of the grand list in this place, and that is, the increasing blows of the many axe-men during the inclement season of the year. Many hundred acres within the last decade, have been swept of wood and timber, till but few acres of old growth remain; perhaps it would not be stating it too strongly, if we were to say that within this period, a full hundred thousand dollars worth of this kind of property has been disposed of in this time.

On the Rutland road just above where Simon G. Harrington now lives, settled one Samuel Brown who came from Sudbury. He had a son, Abel Brown, who was for many years the Town Clerk, who held that office longer than has any person before or since. Of course the personal history of this town officer is obscure at this late day, but we have the right to assume that he must have been a man of superior fitness for the important post which he held so many years. He married a Miss —— Howe, sister of John Howe. He had children—Samuel, 2nd, Augustus and Paul. The second son removed to New Hampshire, while the third went to Cincinnati, where, it is supposed, he perished during the yellow fever scourge which soon after prevailed in that city. Samuel, 2d, remained in town and married Lucretia Earle, daughter of Marmaduke Earle, and had children, viz: John Barnes, Sally, Betsey, Patty, Aurelia, and Matilda. John Barnes Brown married Eliza Chittenden.

Elijah Brown, who came from Westboro, was of another family, he had children—Nathaniel, Sylvester, Elijah, Abi, Mary, Hattie and Fannie. Of these, Sylvester remained with his father, and was never married. They were men of some means, and for many years they owned and kept the "old tavern" at the corner of the Barre and New Braintree roads. This old tavern has witnessed many changes and many a strange event in its day, and a detailed history of it and of those townspeople who frequented it, would make a volume of vivid interest, whether profitable or not. Austin Flagg for many years held forth here as "mine host," and in the days even when the new Barre road had been opened up, and Genery Twitchell held the ribbons of the fast stage line between Brattleboro and Worcester, this old hotel was historic, and yet its glory had not departed, since it was still the place of general rendezvous for all the country round. The amount of ancient flip dispensed here would likely, if let loose at one time, make as great a "washout" as did the great flood of Aug. 19, 1887, when all the highways were terribly torn up.

In the last quarter of a century it has gone to gradual decay and as a hotel abandoned, though it has served as a shoemaker's shop and in the old ell a store was continued for a period. Here Thos. A. Prouty and Aaron Snow did business and were among the last of the thrifty tenants of this house of "ye olden time."

David Manning carried on boot manufacturing here quite extensively up to about 1850. His shop was in what is now the Holmes' house. He lived opposite.

Thomas A. Prouty came here about 1850, from Spencer, and opened a store in the house now owned and occupied by John Holmes, with a boot shop in the upper story. His brother, I. Lothrop Prouty, was a partner. They continued business at this place for several years, and then bought out the Harrington store and continued till they sold to Nathaniel and William H. Clark. Theodore C. and John Prouty also came here and engaged in trade and manufactured boots. They all married their wives here. Thos. A. Prouty married Miss Ellen Pike, Isaac L. Prouty married Miss Mary Skinner, John Prouty married Miss Sarah Jane Bullard, and Theodore C. Prouty married Miss Hannah Peirce. The Prouty brothers remained ten years or so and then returned to Spencer and entered the boot and shoe business, where they have all accumulated fortunes. They were men of unusual shrewdness and great natural ability.

George Rowell was engaged in boot manufacturing at one time, as was also Bigelow, Mulligan & Co. These firms were not long engaged before abandoning the business.

At the present time there are two stores in town, kept by Nathaniel Clark & Co. and Elisha Arnold. The post-office is at Clark's store. The predecessors of the Clarks were, first, the Prouty Brothers, then the Harringtons, a Mr. Brewer and Harvey Wilson. The building itself was erected by Sylvester Brown. As many as five different stores have been established at different times, viz: that of the Browns at the old tavern, Tyler Goddard's, opposite his house on the west side of the road, that of Samuel Jennison's at his mills, also Otis Peirce's, where W. I. Preston now lives, and Thomas A. Prouty's, before mentioned.

In those brisk and changeful days, the trade and travel through this town was considerable. Railroads had not been invented 35 or 40 years ago, or had not superseded the common roads. There was ere long another tavern, known as the "Summit House," kept and owned for many years by Wm. W. Dodd, a large three story building, put up to accommodate the public, and there was need of it. It was no uncommon thing for a dozen four and six horse teams, carrying goods inland from Worcester and Boston to Barre and Brattleboro and all intermediate points, stopping for the night here. Then four and six horse coaches passed and repassed daily, carrying crowds of passengers with the government mails, making it merry as they bowled along over what was then one of the great inland arteries of trade and travel. The advent of the iron horse has changed all this, and now but a single two horse coach goes up and down once a day connecting with the world outside.

There is still an opportunity for the town to make some development in the future in the direction of furnishing accommodations for summer visitors. Already quite a large number frequent the place during the warm season, and when we consider the elevation, good air and reasonable charges, we may confidently hope for some prosperity in this direction.

The elevation above the sea at the "Common" is about eleven hundred and thirty-five feet, Asnebumskit Pond eleven hundred and eight feet, Arnold's Pond eleven hundred and twenty-two feet.

The State has granted a charter giving the right to take Arnold's or Kettle brook to supply a portion of Leicester with water. Surveys have been made the past year looking towards that purpose, but whether any thing is likely to result we are not sufficiently informed to determine. The elevation of Leicester Hill above the sea is given us as one thousand and one foot, thus indicating that it is a feasible project to take the water.

The salubrity of the climate here is pretty well established, and many people have attained to a great age here. Among these we recall the case of Mrs. Jason Livermore, who was one hundred years old at her decease, Mrs. Joseph Penniman and John P. Metcalf were old people; Mrs. Elizabeth Harrington, mother of Deacon Samuel Harrington, died June 27, 1835, at the age of one hundred years and eight months. The Rev. James D. Farnsworth preached at her house on the 31st October, 1834, the day she was one hundred years old, from the text found in Gen. 47 : 9.

There have been more golden weddings celebrated in this town within about ten years, we apprehend, than in any other community of like population in the same period in New England. Among those who have thus celebrated we recall the following : Mr. and Mrs. Silas D. Harrington, Mr. and Mrs. Tyler S. Penniman, Mr. and Mrs. David Harrington, Mr. and Mrs. J. O. Keep, Mr. and Mrs. William B. Rogers, and Mr. and Mrs. John Holmes, two others have passed the fiftieth mile stone but did not celebrate, viz : Mr. and Mrs. J. Barnes Brown, and Mr. and Mrs. Oliver Goodnow.

In 1840 there was great political excitement all over the country, and especially here in New England, and the old log cabin campaign of Harrison so engrossed public attention as to claim much of the time of the country in the way of attending the rallies and listening to addresses that were taking place everywhere. Worcester was to have a great demonstration beyond anything before undertaken, and Daniel Webster was to give an address and the country towns were ablaze with excitement. Several of the back towns, as Barre and Petersham, sent many of their people, who went in marching order, and in this column Paxton joined, and they turned out, as report has it, in great number on foot, in carriages, and very many on horseback—the whole procession being more than a mile in length, and thus reinforced the great column, proceeded to Worcester under the command of Captain Freeman Ellis of Paxton, a prominent citizen, who was the chief marshal of the procession. This Captain Ellis has a son, Wm. F. Ellis, living in this town.

A few items of interest, connected with some of the earlier inhabitants, is herewith appended.

In 1843, Capt. Freeman Ellis was living on Crocker Hill, in the old Bigelow mansion. Captain Ellis was largely engaged in butchering and handling of cattle, and was known to have considerable funds at times about his person on returning from the city. He was returning home one evening, and when in the vicinity of Wilson's woods, he was suddenly accosted by a man who, failing to catch the bridle reins, demanded a ride, but Capt. Ellis put the whip to his horses and got away; the man fired and put a ball through the rear end of the wagon. The highwayman proved afterwards to be, on his own confession, the noted Larned, a member of a gang of bank robbers.

The Crocker house above named, built by the Rev. Silas Bigelow in 1768-9 and in which he died, also where Esquire Nathaniel Crocker used to live and which Rev. Jos. D. Fansworth occupied, was burned in 1844, on the day the "Millerites" set for the world to be destroyed, and concerning which much excitement was afoot.

On page 56, we have spoken of the Howes; Paul Howe, son of John, had three sons, viz: John, Jonah and Jonathan. Jonah Howe, sr. settled on Howe's Hill, now Davis's Hill. There was nothing but a bridle path leading over it to the mills of Newton at the time and for many years afterwards. John lived at his father's, while Jonathan lived at the old Brewery place. Jonah, sr., had sons, Jonah jr. and Artemas. The latter became quite a public man, and had a conspicuous place in town affairs and held various town offices. An anecdote is related of him that one Sunday, during a presidential canvas, the minister preached a sort of political sermon, at the close of which Mr. Howe rose and addressing the preacher, said that "you may vote for whom you are a mind to, I shall vote for Cass if I am alive." He married Miss Roxa Moore, daughter of Pliny Moore, and lived at the Moore homestead, on the Rutland road, just beyond Francis Keep's. This place was subsequently owned by the town as a town farm, till the old Dwight Estabrook farm, on the Barre road was purchased, which latter is the present town farm. The Moore place above named was the home of Capt. Phineas Moore and of Major Willard Moore, who fell at Bunker Hill. It is not known that he was ever married. He had not attained middle life at the time of his death. The Moores have left a reputation equalled by few of the earlier settlers in this town.

Not many years since, while celebrating the fourth of July, a premature discharge of a cannon blew off the arm of one Henry Skinner, which speedily terminated the festivities. On another similar occasion, of recent date, two men very narrowly escaped with their lives.

In ye olden times it was customary to indulge in turkey shooting whenever any considerable company of men assembled. This amusement was usually located not far from some hostelry, and this place had its quota of fun in this direction. The locality where the targets were set up was back of the blacksmith shop of one Samuel Chickering. After 1828 William Stockwell was the blacksmith, and later on Luke Stratton and then Charles Muzzy kept it. This shop was near the place where Luke Stratton now lives. It was in the low lands behind this shop that the crack shots assembled, and this amusement terminated with an accident which we need not relate. Whether the sport of rifle shooting or the taste of old Elijah Brown's popular flip was the most attractive, it is not our duty to say, but one thing is certain, the ancient business of rifle practice never flourished outside of the *range* of an old time country inn.

Several distressing accidents have occured in the past which perhaps should be related. A man who lived in Spencer attempted one winter to cross Asnebumskit Pond on horseback, but the ice proved too thin, both horse and rider were drowned. Soon after, Ithamar Bigelow was passing that way, and observing a hat on the ice, made an investigation and found them and recovered the body of the man. The unfortunate man's name has not been given us.

On August 3, 1865, Albert Browning, son of Richardson Browning, was drowned in the same pond, and William Earle recovered the body by diving.

In 1850, on the fifth of July, Edward Howe, son of Phineas M. Howe, was drowned in Bottomly Pond. Later a young lad was drowned in this pond under circumstances somewhat suspicious, but the inquest did not result in the authorities taking any action in the premises.

Mr. Samuel Slade, who lived at the Slade place, on Dodd's hill, was out drawing wood to the house, and the way being uneven and the load not well balanced, it overturned and Mr. Slade was killed. It was a very unfortunate affair.

There have been several notable storms in this vicinity within the past few years, which deserve mention, because of their severity. In 1871, June 11, a whirlwind or great cyclone appeared, and was so violent as to twist trees from their base and crush others to kindling wood, leveled barns and buildings in its track and roared as it went onward so as to be heard miles away. Its track, a few rods in width only, was across the northerly side of the town and was very destructive.

In 1887, August 19, it begun to rain early in the forenoon. The clouds were dark and threatening. There was no wind accompanying, nor was there thunder or lightning preceding or during the storm, which was of short duration—lasting from 8 A. M. to 1 P. M. But the water that fell in that brief period was towards three inches. It seemed to come in sheets by times, and must have equalled the tropical rain falls experienced by Du Challu in Africa. The empty streams and brooks sprang to surging torrents and dashed wildly towards the valleys and the sea. The highways were practically wrecked for a time and travel over them was well nigh suspended. It took many days' labor to repair damages. The country road to Worcester was impassable for ten days thereafter. The worst place being just this side of Tatnuck, on what is known as "watering-trough hill."

The last great storm was the "blizzard" in March, 1888. The wind settled into the north-east, snowing and blowing briskly from the start and constantly increasing in force till eighty miles an hour was reached in some localities. By the middle of the afternoon the roads were substantially blocked and travel suspended. It was then evident that it was getting perilous to be out even a short distance from home. The next morning fences were invisible, the highways level full, and no mails came or went for three days, and the only sure method of reaching your neighbor was on snow shoes, which were used by some who possessed them. The thermometer kept at about 30° above zero fortunately, and but for this many lives would have been lost in this region.

Of clubs or societies in town there have been several, but of them all, only one continues, and even that has nearly ceased be on several occasions, but easily recuperates and lives on, and this is the Lyceum. It was started about twenty-five years ago and is now in a flourishing condition. It aims to meet fortnightly during the season of long evenings. The temporary organization was effected on February 20, 1864, by choice of Solon C. Howe as Chairman and J. C. Bigelow as Secretary. Subsequently a permanent organization was completed by the choice of William Mulligan, a very active and able man, as President, and J. C. Bigelow as Secretary. No date is given to this meeting. There had been originally about twenty-five names appended to a paper looking to the establishment of a lyceum—this paper was dated February 15, 1864. But the first question up for discussion was at a meeting on March 2, 1864. This and the previous two meetings, to complete the organization, were held in the store of Otis Peirce, who lived and kept store where W. I. Preston now lives, being the first house south of M. B. Olmstead's blacksmith shop. Such a society is a very useful appendage in all communities when well conducted and its mission of instruction and amusement strictly adhered to. Of those prominent in starting the Lyceum was William Mulligan, who was a bright, stirring man and who held many offices of trust and honor in the town. Messrs. Edward S. Burnette, Oliver Goodnow, Simon G. Harrington, John Holmes, Henry Allen, and others were likewise prominent.

In this connection it is proper not to overlook another society, which was a forerunner of the Lyceum and which indeed may be said to have been its progenitor. This was the "Band of Hope," organized July 21, 1860, with Oliver Goodnow as Superintendent. There were more than a hundred members including honoraries, and they met in the central school house. It was at first intended for very young people, and was a semi-religious society, with declamations and singing. In March, 1863, the society changed its name to one more in accord with its work, viz: "The Paxton Speaking and Singing Club," with Willard A. Earle as President and Clara P. Conant as Secretary. This society held meetings as the Lyceum now does, during the season of long evenings. Finally, about Jan. 1, 1864, its name was changed to the "Literary Encampment." At last the older folks, who had become interested in these exercises and in which they had borne a part, decided to establish a Lyceum, as we have seen, which was done within sixty days after the date last above given.

The Ladies Social Union is likewise an important factor in all church affairs here, and should be mentioned. Mrs. Mary A. Boynton was, we believe, the first president, while Mrs. Nathaniel Clark is the present head. Of its secretaries, Miss Ella Rowell, now deceased, is deserving of much credit for the unselfish interest she brought to bear, not only with the Union, but with every worthy movement in town. She was especially devoted to the cause of temperance, and usually took an active part in the gospel temperance meetings. Mr. Edward S. Burnette, who has more constantly and for a longer period than any other person, attended these meetings, says of her, that she was one of the pillars, not only of the temperance cause, but of the church as well.

Another institution of our town flourished about 1840, it was the "Paxton Brass Band," with Thomas Ward as leader. The other members as far as they can now be recalled, were J. Buckley Grosvenor, Oliver Goodnow, Buckley Abbott, George W. Dodd, Horace Peirce, Edward Peirce, Daniel Peirce, Nelson Wood, Samuel Grosvenor, J. B. Brown, Joseph Allen, Willard Abbott, D. Estabrook, —— Spaulding, —— Phillips, and others. This band continued for ten years or more, and became well-known throughout the county. It played in Worcester on invitation of the authorities, one Fourth of July, and was highly spoken of by all who heard them. Again at Fitchburg during the great muster there, they won golden opinions and took the palm over all the other bands in competition, and there were quite a number from other places in the county.

"The Grand Army of the Republic" is a society of comparatively recent organization, and while there is no established Post in this town, its principal officers reside here, and we should fail in our duty if we neglected to chronicle something concerning it. The place of meeting is at Rutland, and three towns are embraced by Post 136, viz: Oakham, Paxton, and Rutland. Its members are composed of Union soldiers residing in these towns. Of its officers at the present time, residing in this town, are George A. Brown, *Commander;* Wm. M. Warren, *Surgeon;* F. T. Merriam, *O. G.*

A descendant of old Dr. John Snow says: "It is the people that make a town, and Paxton has been a grand old town. Have you any idea how many men who have made a mark in the world were born in Paxton? They are to be found all over the country, and though Paxton is small, yet it is these same country towns that are furnishing the brains for our cities." Thus speaks Dr. Windsor N. Snow, and what he states is true to a greater extent than most people believe. His statement reminds us of the high character and great business ability of his ancestor, Col. Willard Snow who built the house where the writer now lives, and likewise many others in town. Of these strong, brainy men of the early days, Maj. Willard Moore was a good example. He promptly left for the seat of war and was promoted for his great gallantry, and finally fell with Warren on the field of Bunker Hill. His brothers, Capt. Ephraim Moore and Lieut. Pliney Moore, were influential men. Then there was Capt. Ralph Earle, who lived where Tyler S. Penniman now lives. The struggle for liberty was about to begin, had in fact already begun, and the royalist party with Gov. Hutchinson at their head in civil power, made every effort to strengthen the hands of the government in these provinces, and to this Ralph Earle he tendered a captain's commission, who spurned the proffered honor. His love of liberty was too deeply seated to be purchased by imperial power, all of his sympathies were with the people in their desire for separation. Gen. Washington, learning of the facts, sent Capt. Earle, who, up to this time, had been only a captain of the militia, a commission as captain in the Continental Army, and from that time on till near the close of the war, he performed active and important service.

Then there were the Davises, Lieut. Simon Davis and Col. John Davis, an uncle, we believe, of "Honest John Davis," who represented Massachusetts in the U. S. Senate with great ability and distinction. Col. John Davis lived where Charles D. Boynton now lives, in the easterly part of the town.

We have already spoken of Revs. Silas Bigelow and Daniel Grosvenor, Dr. Samuel Stearns and Dr. A. J. Howe, Hon. George W. Livermore, and of his noted patriot grandfather, Jason Livermore, also, of Rev. and Hon. John D. Peirce and Rev. Elbridge G. Howe.

Esquire Buddyll Livermore was a well-known and influential man, as was his son, Buddyll Livermore, jr.; and then we recall James Day, Esq., college bred, a careful, painstaking man, perhaps plain spoken, but a man of mark here, and would have been anywhere. Then we should mention Drs. Thaddeus Brown, Samuel Forrest, Caleb Shattuck who practiced medicine here the last part of the eighteenth century; Esquire Jonathan P. Grosvenor, Dr. Absalom Russell, Dr. Thaddeus Amidon, and Dr. Loami Harrington who is reputed as a very skillful physician; Esquire Nathaniel Crocker was also highly prominent and tied more nuptial knots in this town than any civil magistrate before or since. His granddaughter, Reliance Crocker, daughter of Solomon Crocker, married Dea. Edward Kendall of Paxton, now living in Cambridge, and is an eminent man in that place and a warm friend of the church and people here. Tyler Goddard we have mentioned in another place. He represented this town nine consecutive terms in the Legislature. Then there was Thomas Bancroft, brother of Hon. George Bancroft lived here, and was a celebrity. He was a learned man and very genial and always courtly. He will be long remembered.

William Stockwell, who kept a blacksmith shop at one time was a very expert mechanic. He devoted much of his time to making rifles, and had he given strict attention to business he might have become famous perhaps, but he was prone to wander and went away to Canada.

Capt. John Partridge was a singularly able man, and possessed of a great memory and sound common sense. For many years he held some responsible town office, and while an active partisan, he was respected by all classes.

Ralph Earle Bigelow, of the firm of Lakin & Bigelow, was the most eminent of the local business men the town has ever had. He attained to great wealth, and built up a large business. His death was a sad one. He was drowned in Bottomly Pond on July 4, 1873.

George S. Lakin, of the firm of Lakin & Bigelow, sold out and removed to Holden, where he died.

Col. John Brigham was an energetic and forceful man, but he was subsequently environed by some troubles and it is not known where he died. Lawson Ball, as will be remembered, was an eccentric character in his day. He deposited the first ballot in the cause of abolition in this town. Dr. John Frink, jr., was the son of Dr. John Frink of Rutland, and grandson of the Rev. Thomas Frink also of Rutland, where he was ordained in 1827; they were all reputed to be very learned men. Then too there were Capt. Browning Hubbard, father of Hammond W. Hubbard, Dea. Oliver Witt, David, Moses, and Nathaniel Waite, Clark Earle, Stephen and Aaron Coggswell, John and Francis Washburne, John Warren, Abijah Burnap, Jonathan and Dana Frost, Alpheus and Joel Stratton. It was Joel Stratton's influence and timely word that was the cause of John B. Gough's reformation. He lived where Frank A. Peirce now lives. There were also these of equal or even greater prominence in the early and later times—Dea. Silas and Windsor Newton, Moses Parkhurst, Marmaduke Earle, who was a a real patriarch among men, Deacons Samuel and Samuel D. Harrington, Oliver Wilson, Ezra and David Boynton, Abram Livermore, William Duncan, Jude Jones, Stephen Streeter, Hezekiah Newton, Frederick Flint, Alpheus Bemis, William Stockwell, J. Dickerman Newton, who lived on the old Newton farm where David Harrington lived and died, Thaddeus Estabrook, Austin Flagg, Nathaniel Lakin, Joseph Penniman, Daniel Estabrook, Jotham Parker, Simon G. Harrington, William Comins, T. M. Duncan, David Manning, who married Lucy B. Grosvenor, the granddaughter of Rev. Daniel Grosvenor,

Silas D. Harrington, and Dwight Estabrook, sr., all stirring and able men.

We would not forget the skilled physicians, who at various times in later days, have been residents here, and who were skillful in the practice of their profession, viz: Drs. Bellows, Earle, and Addison Knights who built the house where L. T. Kirby lives, Dr. Edward M. Wheeler, Dr. John N. Murdock, Dr. Ambrose Eames, and Dr. George O. Warner. The latter was the last physician who lived in this place. He was a native of Sturbridge, and settled here till after a few years he removed to Leicester, but practiced here up to the time of his decease. He died quite suddenly in Leicester of diphtheria, in 1886, beloved beyond most men in this community. Many of the foregoing are worthy of more extended biographical mention.

In the notice of the Church on page 22, the name of Hezekiah Newton is omitted from the list of the earliest church members. It is singular that all of the names given in that list should be males; three days after the organization the wives of most of them joined. Sixteen others joined the first year and thirteen the second and last year of Rev. Mr. Bigelow's ministry. Mr. Bigelow, leaving the farm house of his brother, Ithamar, set about erecting a parsonage on the height of land then known as Bigelow Hill, now Crocker. The house was a square structure, of the style and size of the Goddard house now standing. Mr. Bigelow took a severe cold on Oct. 21, 1769, while superintending the completion of his new home, and died Nov. 16, following. This place was subsequently owned and occupied by Nathaniel Crocker,

Esq. At the time the house was burned it was occupied by Capt. Freeman Ellis.

The following persons have held the office of Deacon in the Church, viz : Oliver Witt, Ephraim Moore, Timothy Barrett, David Davis, Jonah Howe, sr., Abel Brown, Nathan Swan, Samuel Harrington, David Davis, jr., Samuel D. Harrington, Silas N. Grosvenor, John Conant, William Conant, John B. Moore, Josiah O. Keep, William B. Rogers, William Brown, Wm. H. Harrington, and Levi Smith.

Up to 1830-3, there were less than a dozen dwellings in what is now known as the village proper. These houses were the the old Lakin house, the old yellow house, the Crow Hill house, and the house nearly opposite, now occupied by Luke Stratton, Capt. John Partridge's, now used as a hotel and kept by M. B. Olmstead, the house of the late Silas D. Harrington, now occupied by D. C. Stratton, Brown's Hotel, the Goddard and Bigelow (Crocker) mansions. At the present time, there are forty-six in the village, and yet the population of the town is less than at the date last mentioned.

On May 1, 1888, the number of polls assessed was 145. The value of personal estate owned was $35,375.00 ; value of buildings, $99,050.00 ; lands were valued at $148,008.00. Rate of taxation was $12.60 per thousand. The number of horses 121, cows 288, other neat stock 167, sheep 24, swine 43, number of dwelling houses 138, acres of land 8,643.

List of persons who enlisted for longer or shorter terms of time during the war. Some of the number re-enlisted, thus counting twice on the town's quota, and two were drafted.

HENRY A. ALLEN, served two enlistments,
SIMON C. ABBOTT,
EDWARD D. BIGELOW,
HENRY G. BIGELOW,*
GEORGE R. BROWNING, re-enlisted,
HENRY A. BROWNING, died of wounds,
CHARLES A. BEMIS,*
CHARLES S. BUTLER,
JAMES D. BUTLER,* died June, 1865,
CHARLES G. BIGELOW, served two enlistments,
WILLIAM F. BROWNING,   "   "   "
ISAAC J. BOWEN,
HENRY A. W. BLACKBURN,
GEORGE W. BROWN,* died in 1864,
GEORGE P. BROWNING,
GEORGE F. CHENEY,*
HERBERT CHENEY,
DANIEL CUMMINGS, died April 28, 1862,
JOHN A. CUMMINGS,
EVERETT W. CONANT,
WALLACE S. CHASE,
WILLIAM P. DAVIS,
OTIS DAMON, re-enlisted,
GEORGE W. DODD, Commissioned as Lieut.
ALANSON H. DODGE,
AMBROSE EAMES,
ORWELL J. GOODNOW,
ALWIN S. GRATON,
CHARLES E. GRATON,*

James Holmes,
Michael Kerrigan,
Sylvester Larrabee,
Nathan A. Munroe, died in Tenn., Aug. 8, 1862,
Solomon R. Maynard, died at Newport News, March 2, 1863.
Edward E. Munroe, died while a prisoner,
Frank W. Mulligan,
John S. Mills, died at Washington, April 15, 1865.
Alvin S. Nichols, died in Tenn.
Samuel A. Newton,
Nahum S. Newton,
Erastus W. Newton,
Charles H. Newton,
Cyprus Osland, died May 4, 1862.
Edward F. Pratt,
David W. Pratt, died at Andersonville, 1864.
John S. Pratt,   "   "   "   "
Albert Pratt,
George O. Peirce, died at Harrison Landing, Va., July, 1862.
John D. Peirce, killed at Petersburg, Va.
Hollis H. Howe, died at Yorktown in 1862.
Charles A. Harrington, died at Annapolis, Jan. 8, 1862.
Ward Harris,
Samuel Harrington,
George M. Harris,
John Holmes, Jr.
George R. Hubbard, killed in the trenches at Petersburg,

William E. Keep, served two enlistments.
William F. Pike,
Hiram N. Parkhurst, died at Newbern, Sept. 1864.
Charles H. Parker,
Walter Shaw, died at Washington in 1862.
Samuel Stratton,* died Sept. 6, 1864.
Isaac R. Savage,
John W. Smith,
William Ware,
Henry C. Ward,
William M. Warren,
Benjamin F. Ware,*
John K. Davis, } drafted men.
William Gibson, (colored,)
Henry Evans, substitute.
Barney Hastings, and one other enlisted by the State were credited on our quota.

Of this number 25 are reported as born in Paxton. Those marked thus * enlisted elsewhere.

List of Names upon the Soldiers' Monument.

Henry A. Browning,
Daniel Cummings,
Solomon R. Maynard,
John S. Mills,
Alvin S. Nichols,
Edward E. Munroe,
James D. Butler,
George R. Hubbard,
Samuel W. Stratton,
George W. Brown,

Hiram N. Parkhurst,
John S. Pratt,
David W. Pratt,
Nathan A. Munroe,
Samuel G. Osland,
George O. Peirce,
John D. Peirce,
Hollis H. Howe,
Charles A. Harrington,
Walter Shaw,

Hezekiah Sargent.

THE HISTORY OF PAXTON. 95

This monument is a plain granite shaft, situated near the centre of the "Common." It was erected about eighteen years ago at a cost of eight hundred dollars. Of this sum the town granted five hundred, and the other three hundred dollars was by private subscription. The Ladies' Social Union caused the iron fence to be placed around the mound and shaft. This was done at an expense of about three hundred dollars. The four large cannon were procured from the general government through the assistance of Hon. W. W. Rice, on the petition of the writer and others. The whole effect of this simple shaft is in keeping with its surroundings, and is a fitting memorial of those who fell in the conflict of 1861.

Here we bring this brief history to a close, trusting that it may at least serve as a foundation for a more extended work in the future.

SUPPLEMENT.

The genealogy of some of the first settlers of the town and their descendants is given here. Other families would have been published had we had time to have gathered the necessary data or had it been furnished to us.

The genealogies of the Harrington, Peirce and Brown families are largely given in the preceding pages.

THE ABBOTTS.

ABIJAH ABBOTT, b. April 14, 1756, d. April 10, 1810. Rachel his wife, b. Dec. 18, 1759. They had children:

    AARON, b. Sept. 20, 1780, d. Jan. 1832.
    LOIS.
    DANIEL.
    ABIJAH, JR.
    PATTY, m. Charles Lamb.
    SUSIE, m. Mr. MacLane.

AARON ABBOTT, m. Betsey Howe, she was born Nov. 28, 1785, d. Aug. 13, 1865. They had children:

    BETSEY SOPHIA, b. April 13, 1807.
    CHARLES ADDISON, b. July 4, 1809, d. July 31, 1811.
    CHARLES BUCKLEY, b. Sept. 22, 1811.
    LUCY HUBBARD, b. Nov. 13, 1813.
    SAMUEL JENNINGS, b. Dec. 23, 1816, d. Sept. 29, 1821.

ABIGAIL MARIETTA, b. Dec. 27, 1818.
CLARISA HOWE, b. Oct. 24, 1820.
NANCY CLARK, b. Sept. 29, 1822.
SIMON CHENEY, b. Feb. 28, 1825.

THE BOYNTONS.

EBENEZER BOYNTON, b. 1742, came from Sudbury, married PERSIS FAY of Holden. He died July 26, 1815. She died Dec. 4, 1817. They had children:
PERSIS, b. Feb. 21, 1769.
EBENEZER, JR., b. Nov. 10, 1770.
SILAS, b. May 17, 1772.
JEREMIAH, b. June 22, 1774.
ALPHEUS, b. Dec. 17, 1775.
PHEBE, b. Sept. 15, 1778.
LEVI, b. Oct. 18, 1779.
HANNAH, b. Nov. 20, 1781.
ASA, b. April 20, 1783.
DAVID, b. Dec. 11, 1784.
EZRA, b. Oct. 18, 1786.
WILLIAM, b. June 18, 1789.
REUBEN, b. July 4, 1791.
SAMUEL, b. Feb. 15, 1793.

EZRA BOYNTON, b. ――――, m. Phebe Davis, the daughter of Col. John Davis and Phebe Stearns. They had children:
CHARLES DAVIS, b. July 25, 1812.
HANNAH GATES, b. Jan. 31, 1819.
PHEBE STEARNS, b. June 20, 1822,
PERSIS FAY, b. Nov. 16, 1828.

DAVID BOYNTON, b. ―――― m. Lucy B. Johnson of Worcester. They had a large family, viz:

Lucy P., b. March 14, 1814.
Mary Ann, b. March 3, 1816.
Darwin Russell, b. March 4, 1818.
Alonzo, b. May 2, 1822.
Alona, b. Jan. 13, 1824.
David, b. Dec. 14, 1825.
Nathan S., b. Sept. 20, 1827.
George D., b. Oct. 1, 1829.
Lewis J., b. Dec. 28, 1831.
Edwin Nelson, b. Dec. 8, 1833.
Clarissa M., b. Feb. 6, 1836.
Austin, b. Jan. 27, 1838.
Ellen J., b. Jan. 28, 1841.

Charles Davis Boynton, m. Mary A. Towne of Charlton, on Dec. 22, 1841. They have no children.

Hannah Gates Boynton, m. Tyler S. Penniman, and have children:
George Davis.
Ellen Elizabeth.
Frank Henry.

Persis Fay Boynton, m. 1st, Sumner Lincoln, 2nd, Tyler Clough of Brookfield.

Darwin R. Boynton, m. 1st, Nancy Stowe, April, 1846; m. 2nd, Mary Ann Gould. No chidren.

THE BIGELOW FAMILY.

Rev. Silas Bigelow, b. 1739, and came from Concord and Shrewsbury, it is supposed, and was ordained in Paxton, Oct. 21, 1767. He died Nov. 16, 1769, aged thirty years. His wife was Mrs. Sarah Hall of Sutton. Intentions of marriage were published Sept. 22, 1769.

ITHAMAR BIGELOW, b. 1746, m. Persis Barrett, daughter of Dea. Timothy Barrett. He was a brother of the Rev. Silas Bigelow. Died March 16, 1807. He lived on Asnebumskit. Had children:
TIMOTHY, b. Oct. 4. 1770, m. Anna Earle 1797.
SILAS, b. ———, d. April 2, 1783.
SILAS, b. Jan. 24, 1772, d. April 10, 1829.
ITHAMAR, JR., b. Nov. 21, 1773.
PERSIS, b. Nov. 15, 1775, m. Joel Smith in 1796.
LUCY, b. April 25, 1778.
LEWIS, b. Sept. 1, 1780, d. Sept. 28, 1807.

ITHAMAR BIGELOW, JR., m. Sophia Earle, daughter of Clark Earle, May 31, 1801. The Rev. Daniel Grosvenor, their pastor, officiating. He died March 27, 1861. She was born June 15, 1777, d. March 20, 1848. They had children:
WALTER RALEIGH, b. April 30, 1802, d.
RALPH EARLE, b. June 14, 18o— d. July 4, 1873.
LEWIS, b. Aug. 31, 1808, d.

WALTER R. BIGELOW, b. April 30, 1802, m. Eliza Mowar, (b. Dec. 25, 1808, d. May 22, 1869.) They had children:
GEORGE CURTIS, b. April 9. 1830, d. May 12, 1859. He married 1st, June 16, 1853, Mary W. Whittemore. Had children: MARY ELIZA, b. July 22, 1854, d. Aug. 6, 1855, m. 2nd, Ellen M. Clifford, Nov. 10, 1857.
SAMUEL THOMAS, b. May 10, 1834, d. June 29, 1879. He married May 20, 1861, Mrs. Ellen M. C. Bigelow. Had children: GEORGE CLIFFORD, b. Dec. 18, 1862, d. Dec. 31, 1881. GRACE MOWAR, b. July 7, 1871. ALICE MURDOCK, b. March 14, 1877.

RALPH EARLE BIGELOW, b. June 14, 1804, d. July 4, 1873, m. 1st, Tryphena Lakin, 2nd, Malona Chaffin. Had children :
    HENRY, b. Oct. 27, 1829.
    CAROLINE H., b. Jan. 17, 1831, m. George W. April 3, 1850.
    EMELINE E., b. April 9, 1833, m. Henry C. Ward.
    JOHN C., b. Sept. 15, 1838. Children by Malona Chaffin. She died Aug. 12, 1869.

JOHN C. BIGELOW, m. Sarah M. Parker, Nov. 14, 1861. Had children :
    FRED. ANDREW, b. Jan. 31, 1868.
    BERTHA LEE, b. Dec. 11, 1871.

LEWIS BIGELOW, m. on April 1, 1833, 1st, Phebe T. Davis, daughter of David Davis, Jr., 2nd, Mrs. Hannah Howard. Had children :
    EDWARD D., b. Nov. 16, 1835.
    CHARLES G., b. Aug. 18, 1839.
    HENRY G., b. Oct. 22, 1842.
    GEORGE LEWIS, b. July 11, 1844.
    ELMINA SOPHIA, one year old, d. Feb. 9, 1848.
    PHEBE M., b. Feb. 24, 1850.
    ELIZA M., b. June 14, 1852.

SILAS BIGELOW, b. in Paxton Feb. 6, 1786, son of Ithamar and Persis (Barrett) Bigelow, m. 1st, Sophia Lamb, June 19, 1816. He died April 10, 1829. Had children by first wife (Sophia Lamb):
    JOHN FLAVEL, b. April 25, 1818.
    ARTEMAS EDWIN, b. Sept. 3, 1819, unmarried.
    ADELINE EULALIA, b. April 27, 1821.
    GEORGE NORMAN, b. Jan. 14, 1823, m. Nov. 25, 1856, 1st, Frances Louisa Babcock, 2nd, Dec. 6, 1866, Fannie Whitcomb.

Nancy Judson, b. Oct. 11, 1824, d. Aug. 25, 1878.
He married for his second wife Adeline Buxton,
June 11, 1826. They had no children.

John Flavel Bigelow, m. Sophronia Nye Lovell,
Aug. 17, 1847. He died June 20, 1884. Had children:
Mary Eliza, b. Dec. 14, 1856, d. Sept. 7, 1859.
Derwent, b. March 29, 1864, m. Mary Platte,
and lives in Brooklyn, N. Y.

Adeline Eulalia Bigelow, m. Ralph Earle, May
15, 1839. Had children:
Sophia Rogers, b. April 12, 1842.
Sophronia Adeline, b. June 5, 1845.

George Norman Bigelow, m. 1st, Frances Louisa
Babcock, Nov. 25, 1856. They had children:
Eulalia Frances, b. Nov. 20, 1857, d. Aug. 17, 1863.
George Norman, Jr., b. Aug. 5, 1861, d. Aug. 18, 1863.
Frances Eulalia, b. May 21, 1863.

He married 2nd, Fannie Whitcomb of Keene, N.
H., Dec. 6, 1866. He died Aug. 28, 1887.

THE EARLE FAMILY.

Ralph[1] Earle came from England, lived for a time
at Newport, but died at Portsmouth, R. I., in 1678.
He married Joan ——. Had children:
Ralph, m. Dorcas Sprague.
William, m. 1st, Mary Walker, 2nd, Prudence ——.
Mary, m. William Corey.
Martha, m. William Wood.
Sarah, m. Thomas Cornell.

WILLIAM [2] EARLE, b. ———, m. 1st, Mary Walker, 2nd, Prudence ———. He died June 15, 1715. He lived in Portsmouth and Dartmouth. His will was executed Nov. 13, 1713. By this will he gave away several slaves to his children. He was a Quaker, as was his father and descendants to a comparatively late date. His children were:

    MARY, b. 1655, m. John Borden.
    WILLIAM, m. Elizabeth ———.
    RALPH, b. 1660, m. Mary Hicks.
    THOMAS, m. Mary Taber.
    CALEB, m. Mary ———.
    PRUDENCE, m. Benjamin Durfee.

RALPH [3] EARLE, son of William [2] m. Mrs. Mary Hicks, daughter of Robert Carr of Newport, R. I. He died 1757, in Leicester, to which place he moved from Dartmouth. He was obliged to use an Indian guide a part of the way, there being no direct path. He bought the tract known as Mulbury Grove, in Leicester. He was a devout Quaker, and once visited Wm. Penn, who became attached to him. He made his will and gave freedom papers to a slave called "Sharp," and gave him thirty acres of land on the South-East face of Asnebumskit. Had children :

    WILLIAM, b. Nov. 12, 1690, m. Anna Howard.
    JOHN, b. April 24, 1692, m. Mrs. Sarah Borden.
    MARY, b. Oct. 24, 1693.
    ELIZABETH, b. Dec. 24, 1696, m. Robert Lawton.
    SARAH, b. Jan. 18, 1698, m. Stephen Manchester.
    MARTHA, b. Dec. 21, 1700.
    PATIENCE, b. Nov. 24, 1703, m. Benjamin Richardson.
    RALPH, b. March 14, 1704.

Robert, b. March 2, 1706, m. 1st, Mary Newhall, 2nd, Hepzibah Johnson.

Mary, b. March 13, 1708, m. Jotham Rice.

Benjamin, b. March 14, 1711, m. 1st, Abigail Newhall, 2nd, Mrs. Deborah Slade.

Robert [4] Earle, son of Ralph, [3] who was the son of William, [2] who was the son of Ralph. [1] Robert had children:

Martha, b. Nov. 3, 1726.
Nathan, b. May 12, 1728.
Mary, b. Aug. 10, 1730.
Elizabeth, b. Oct. 18, 1732.
George, b. March 3, 1735.
Thomas, b. Aug. 27, 1737, m. Hannah Wait.
Ezek, b. Feb. 10, 1741.
Robert, b. Oct. 10, 1743.
Lydia, b. Aug. 15, 1746.
Marmaduke, b. March 8, 1749, m. Elizabeth Newton.
Phebe, b. Dec. 22, 1756.
Timothy, b. March 13, 1759. He died in U. S. Army, Nov. 3, 1777.

Marmaduke [5] Earle, b. in Leicester, March 8, 1749, m. Elizabeth Newton Aug. 14, 1772, daughter of Jonas Newton of Paxton. He died May 29, 1839. He was a Quaker. Was buried in Leicester. Had children:

Lucretia, b. Feb. 25, 1773, m. Samuel Brown, 2nd.
Catherine, b. March 3, 1775, m. Francis Washburn.
Winthrop, b. May 5, 1777, d. Jan. 15, 1836.

DELIVERANCE, b. Nov. 10, 1779, m. Jonathan Cunningham.
SAMUEL, b. Dec. 26, 1781, d. June 21, 1787.
AMASA, b. March 11, 1784, m. Lucy Howe.
PHILIP, b. April 11, 1786, m. Patty Barton.
REBECCA, b. July 21, 1788, m. James Thompson.
EMORY, b. Sept. 10, 1790, m. Eunice Smith.
CANDACE, b. Nov. 3, 1792, m. William Boynton.
PERSIS, b. Nov. 18, 1794, m. Wm. H. Scott.
PHEBE, b. June 22, 1797, m. Moses Parkhurst.
ELMER, b. Jan. 6, 1800, m. Sally Bellows.
Homer, b. May 6, 1802, d. Aug. 30, 1804.

PHILIP [6] DARL, (son of Marmaduke,) b. April 10, 1786, in Paxton, m. June 18, 1807, Patty U. Barton of Leicester. He died in Paxton Jan. 7, 1869. He was a scythe maker. Had children:

ELIZA J., b. April 18, 1808, (m. Samuel Peirce, who died Nov. 8, 1876). She died Oct. 4, 1863. They had Hannah, b. March 30, 1833, who m. T. C. Prouty of Spencer.—Hannah died Feb. 4, 1875 or '6.
WILLIAM BARTON, b. Aug. 28, 1810, m. 1st, Hannah Humes, 2nd, Nancy A. Horton.
SARAH G., b. Sept. 27, 1817, m. D. Gates Davis.

WILLIAM [4] Earle, b. Nov. 12, 1690, m. Anna Howard of R. I. He built a grist mill in Leicester and was one of the earliest members of the Quaker Society in the place. Had children:

WILLIAM, JR., b. April 27, 1714, m. Mary Cutting.
ELIZABETH, b. May 12, 1716, m. John Potter.
MARY, b. Feb. 28, 1719, m. James Lawton, Jr.
DAVID, b. Aug. 16, 1721, m. Martha Earle.
JUDITH, b. Aug. 11, 1723, m. George Cutting.

RALPH, b. Nov. 13, 1726, m. 1st, Phebe Whittemore, July 19, 1750, 2nd, Mrs. Naomi Kinnicutt.

JOHN, b. March 1, 1729.

RALPH [5] EARLE, son of William, [4] b. Nov. 13, 1726, m. 1st, Phebe Whittemore, July 19. 1750, 2nd, Mrs. Naomie Kinnicutt of R. I. He owned the place where Tyler S. Penniman now lives. He died about 1808. He was a very prominent man, and Gov. Hutchinson commissioned him as Captain in the British army in 1776. He declined to accept and was subsequently commissioned by General Washington, as Captain, this he accepted and took an active part in the Revolutionary War. Had children :

RALPH b. May 14, 1751, m. Sarah Gates.
CLARK, b. April 17, 1753, m. ——
ARTEMAS, b. Nov. 28, 1754, d. March 19, 1755.
JAMES, b. May 1, 1761, m. Mrs. C. Smith.
DEXTER, b. Dec. 10; 1776, in Paxton.

CLARK [6] EARLE, son of Ralph [5] and Phebe (Whittemore) Earle, m. 1st, Hepzibah Howard, 2nd, Mrs. Matilda Whittemore Chace, in 1800. They had children :

SOPHIA, b. June 15, 1777.
BETSEY, b. Dec. 4, 1780.
RALPH, b. Jan. 11, 1783.
DEXTER, b. Nov. 7, 1786.
BETSEY HEPZIBAH, b. Dec. 4, 1801.
CAROLINE,—

DEXTER [7] Earle, b. Nov. 7, 1786, d. Nov. 9, 1855, m. Susanna Eaton and had children :

RALPH, b. Nov. 13, 1811.

Sophia B. E., b. Oct. 11, 1813, m. Dea. William B. Rogers.
Lavinnia, b. Sept. 8, 1816, d. ——.
Mary S., b. May 8, 1818.
Clark.
James C.
George, d. Jan. 14, 1864.
Lewis Bigelow, b. April 1830, d. Aug. 16, 1860.

Ralph [8] Earle, b. Nov. 13, 1811, m. Adeline Eulalia Bigelow, (b. April 27, 1821,) daughter of Silas Bigelow, May 15, 1839. Had children:
Sophia Rogers, b. April 12, 1842.
Sophronia Adeline, b. June 5, 1845.

Sophie R. Earle, m. at No.— President Street, Brooklyn, N. Y., Ledyard Bill, son of Gurdon and Lucy (Yerrington) Bill, of Ledyard, Conn., June 12, 1872. They have children:
Frederic Ledyard, b. June 13, 1873.
Bertha Earle, b. June 5, 1875.
Lucy Sophie, b. Oct. 28, 1882.

THE DAVIS FAMILY.

Lieut. Simon Davis came from Concord with his wife Dorothy, to Rutland, as early as 1720, the records say. They had children:

Joseph, Israel, Eleazar, Simon, Martha, Oliver, Mary and Azubah. He died in Holden at the house of his son Eleazar.

Simon Davis, Jr., settled in that part of Rutland, now Paxton, where C. A. Streeter lives. He married Hannah Gates, of Rutland, Sept. 10, 1733. They had children:

Elizabeth, b. Jan.— 1735; Hannah, b. March, 1736; Miram, b. June, 1738; David, b. June, 1739; Elizabeth, b. June, 1742; Simon, b. April, 1744; Mercy, b. June, 1745; Simon, b. Aug., 1747; Isaac, b. Feb., 1749; Samuel, b. June, 1751; John, b. Sept., 1752.
He died April 9, 1754, in Holden.

ISAAC DAVIS, son of Simon Davis, Jr., married a Miss — Brigham, and had John Davis. Isaac Davis died April 27, 1826, in Northboro, where he lived.

JOHN DAVIS, son of Simon, Jr., m. Relief Howe. Had children:
Clarissa, Sophronia, Horatio Gates.

DAVID DAVIS, b. in 1739. Died Feb. 11, 1824, married 1st, Lucy Buckman, 2d, Abigal Brown. He lived near Streeters. Had children:
Simon, b. Sept. 2, 1765; Phebe, b. Feb. 2, 1768; Samuel, b. March 18, 1776; Martha, b. Feb. 10, 1771; David, Jr., b. Sept. 17, 1773; Elias, b. ———; Abigal, b. April 1, 1781.

DAVID DAVIS, JR., married Patty Howe, Nov. 18, 1795. He died Aug. 5, 1852. Had children: (list incomplete).

Abigal Brown, b. April 24, 1799; Lucy Buckman, b. Aug. —, 1801: Sarah Newton, b. May 29, 1804, d. Dec. 23, 1806; David Gates, b. Feb. 21, 1815.

DAVID GATES DAVIS, married Sarah G. Earle, June 11, 1839. She was b. Sept. 27, 1817, daughter of Philip Earle. Had children:

William Philip, b. Jan. 6, 1844, m. M. Jennett Stott, March 30, 1865; Eliza Abigal, b. Dec. 21, 1846; David Davis, b. July 24, 1852; Elias Wyman, b. Aug. 23, 1854; Gilbert Gates, b. Jan. 27, 1859.

THE ESTABROOKS.

JONAH ESTABROOK, came from ——, and settled in Rutland, where he died in ——. He had children:
Daniel.

DANIEL ESTABROOK, b.— m.— and had children: George D., b.

GEORGE D. ESTABROOK, married Dec. 12, 1861, Fannie E. Stratton.

THADDEUS ESTABROOK, b. in 1747, d. in 1818. He married ——. Had children:
John, Tyler and Dwight.

DWIGHT ESTABROOK, b. Jan. 9, 1803, d. Sept. 1842. He married Oct. 5, 1824, Abi Brown, daughter of Elijah Brown. She was born Nov. 2, 1802. They had children:
Dwight, Jr., b. July 6, 1825; Marie Antoinette, b.— she married Luther Goddard and lives in Worcester; Fannie Brown, b.— m. George Brown of Leicester, and now reside in Philadelphia; Daniel Franklin, b.— m.—; Dennis Francis, b.— m.—

DWIGHT ESTABROOK, JR., m. Miss Mary B. Rogers, daughter of Nathan Rogers of Holden, on Aug. 13, 1846. They had children:
Alphonso D., b. Jan. 13, 1847; Arthur F., b. May 6, 1848; Sylvester Brown, b. Nov. 1, 1849; Edison F., b. Nov. 7, 1851; Nathan W., b. Aug. 3, 1853, d. March 5, 1854; Abbie Smith, b. Jan. 5, 1857.

THE FLINTS.

JOHN FLINT, m. Phebe Smith of Paxton, and had son, Frederick, born in Oakham.

FREDERICK FLINT, b. May 24, 1782, m. by Nathaniel Crocker, Esq., to Polly Smith, sister of Mrs. John Howe, Jr., March 10, 1806. He died Dec. 1, 1860. Had children:

Phebe, b. April 3, 1807, m. M. R. Williams, March 15, 1843, d. Feb. 24, 1873; Mary Ann, b. Sept. 24, 1812, m. Levi Jotham, Dec. 1, 1840, d. Nov. 16, 1846; Sarah Jane, b. Nov. 20, 1823, d. March 26, 1845; Austin, b. Aug. 12, 1826, d. March 9, 1858; Charles S., b. Oct. 10. 1817, m.— d. Feb. 19, 1884.

AUSTIN FLINT, m. Hattie Garfield. Had children: Emma L., Fred. A.

CHARLES S. FLINT, m. Mary M. Williams, Oct. 7, 1845. Had children:

Mary Jane, b. June 22, 1849, d. May 22, 1855; Chas. F., b. April 18, 1857, m. Susie E. Wakeford, Jan. 9, 1889.

THE GROSVENORS.

REV. DANIEL GROSVENOR, (the grandson of John Grosvenor, who came to Roxbury at an early date), was born in Pomfret, Conn., about 1751. He married Deborah Hall, daughter of Dr. David Hall of Sutton. They had children:

Daniel Buckley, b. about 1777; David Hall, b. Nov. 31, 1779; Jonathan Prescott, b. Nov. 31, 1779—twins; Deborah Newton, b. about 1781; Ebenezer Oliver, b. about 1783; Lucy Williston, b. about 1785; Ira Rufus, b.— died young; Elizabeth Sophia, b. 1789; Cyrus Pitt, b. 1790; Moses Gill, b. 1792.

JONATHAN PRESCOTT GROSVENOR, m. Bethia Avery in 1804. She was daughter of Rev. Joseph Avery of

Holden, and a grand-neice of Gov. Samuel Adams of Boston. He died Sept. 11, 1854. They had children:
Daniel Prescott, b. June 23, 1805; Mary Avery, b. June, 1806; Joseph Avery, b. Aug. — 1808; Lucy Bethia, b. March 10, 1810; Samuel Avery, b. Dec.— 1815, d. in 1850; Harriet Newell, b. May 5, 1818; Elizabeth Hall, b. June 1820; Jonathan Buckley, b. April — 1822; Sarah Thaxter, b. Dec. — 1824; Chas. William, b. Feb. 14, 1827.

DANIEL PRESCOTT GROSVENOR, m. Harriet Peirce of Paxton, daughter of Job Peirce. They had children:
Martha Peirce, b. in 1829; Edward Peirce, b.—; Harriet Elizabeth, b.—; Daniel Prescott, Jr., b.—.

CYRUS PITT GROSVENOR, graduated from Dartmouth about 1815. He married Mrs. Sarah Warner of New York. They had children:
Sarah Caroline; Emma, d. young; Cyrus Pitt, Jr., d. young.

He was a distinguished clergyman and preached in Utica, N. Y., and in Georgetown, S. C., then in Boston and Salem. In his house in Salem was formed the first Anti-Slavery Society in New England. He was sent as delegate to London in 1840, to attend a great convention there in favor of universal freedom.

MOSES GILL GROSVENOR, m. Sophia Grout of Petersham. Had no children. He was a Congregational minister and preached in Haverhill, and in Keene, N. H. He died in Worcester.

LUCY BETHIA GROSVENOR, m. David Manning, a boot manufacturer in Paxton, on May 17, 1838. They reside in Worcester at this time. They had children:
Bertha Grosvenor, b. Aug. 16, 1840, m. Col. Jos. A.

Titus; George Gilman, b. Oct. — 1842; Theodore, b. Oct. 1844; David, Jr. b. Aug. 29, 1846, m. Miss — Bigelow; Charles Walter, b. Aug. 1848; Joseph Avery, b. Feb. 1851.

CHARLES W. GROSVENOR, m. Nancy Clapp of Holden. He resides in Leicester. They had children:
Samuel Avery, Jonathan Prescott, Clarence Willie, David Clapp, Ella Elizabeth, Addie Maria.

JONATHAN BUCKLEY GROSVENOR, m. Sarah Jane Lattimer of Hartford, Conn. They had children:
Mary Avery, Grace G.

ELIZABETH GROSVENOR, b.—, m. Isaac D. White and live in Brookline. Had children:
Isaac D., Jr., Carrie, Grace, Frances, Mary Avery.

SAMUEL AVERY GROSVENOR, b.—, m.—. Had children:
Lewis.

HARRIET NEWELL GROSVENOR, m. Daniel W. Kent of Leicester. Had children:
Lucy, Ruth A., Prescott Grosvenor, Hattie E., Carrie E. and Daniel.

THE HOWE FAMILY.

JOHN HOWE, b. Sept. 16, 1682, d. May 19, 1754. He came from Marlboro to Paxton. He had son.

PAUL HOWE, b. June 18, 1715. He m. Elizabeth Howe of Marlboro and died in 1765. She died Feb. 5, 1807, aged 87. Had children:

John Howe, m.—; Jonah Howe, b. 1746, m. Sarah Newton and d. Nov. 10, 1832; Jonathan, b.—, never married and lived at the "Old Brewery" place. He d. Feb. 27, 1835.

JOHN HOWE, 2nd, son of Paul, m. Lucy ——. Had children :
Paul, 2nd, b.— ; Charles, b.— ; Samuel Hubbard, b.— ; Lucy, b. Dec. 16, 1782, m. Amasa Earle in 1804 ; John, Jr., b. Feb. 16, 1784 ; Betsey, b. Nov. 28, 1785, m. Aaron Abbott in 1806, Nov. 15 ; Delia, b. June 16, 1788 ; Dulcina, b. Aug. 10, 1800 ; Salibity, b.— ; Hollis H., b. Oct. 19, 1802 ; Nancy, b.— ; Solon C., b. Nov. 9, 1804 ; George Buckley, b. Aug. 4, 1806.

JOHN HOWE, JR., b. Feb. 16, 1784, m. Lucy Smith, Jan. 1, 1807, and settled on Brigham Hill. They had children :
J. Orris, b.— ; Abram ; Jarvis, b.—; Lucy ; Augusta Maria, b. Sept. 15, 1807 ; Aaron, Lucy, Maria, Solon C.

JONAH HOWE, son of Paul, 1st, b. 1746, d. Nov. 10, 1832, m. Sarah Newton, daughter of Silas Newton, and lived on Howe's Hill. Had children :
Rufus, b. Jan. 4, 1772 ; Jonah, Jr., b. April 22, 1774 ; Patty, b. March 16, 1776, m. David Davis, Jr. ; Alice, b. March 21, 1779 ; Sally, b. May 12, 1781 ; Artemas, b. Sept. 20, 1783 ; Richardson, b.— ; Relief, b. July 21, 1789 ; Lavinnia, b. June 7, 1791, m. Abram Livermore ; Clarissa, b. May 16, 1794 ; Catherine, b.

ARTEMAS HOWE, above, m. Roxa Moore, b. April 7, 1785, daughter of Pliny Moore. He d. Oct. 12, 1854. They lived on the Rutland road at the Moore Homestead, afterwards the town farm, near Francis Keep's place. They had children :
Phineas Moore, b. June 8, 1808, d. May 30, 1881 ; Jonah, b. Dec. 24, 1810 ; Pliny K., b. April 12, 1813 ; Artemas, Jr., b. Oct. 12, 1815 ; Hannah D., b. Jan. 27, 1819 ; Roxa M., b. Oct. 13, 1821 ; Z. Swift Moore, b. June 6, 1824.

JONAH HOWE, JR., b. April 22, 1774, m. Lydia Warren Sept.—, 1796, and lived a few rods west of his father. They had children:
Benjamin F., b. Sept. 21, 1797; Elbridge Gerry, b. Aug. 14, 1799; Willard, b. Oct. 6, 1801; Rachel W., b. Oct. 24, 1803; Tirza, b. April 30, 1805; Porter, b. April 30, 1807, d. June 12, 1807.

ELBRIDGE GERRY HOWE, son of Jonah, Jr., m. for his 2nd wife, Mary Soule Sturtevant. He died about 1883, at Waukegan, Ill. They had children:
Elbridge Gerry, b. Aug. 22, 1863; Ira Sturtevant, b. Jan. 31, 1866.

J. ORRIS HOWE, son of John Jr., b. Jan. 17, 1810, m. Maria Elizabeth Maynard, b. Dec. 23, 1825, of Marlboro, and lives on Brigham Hill. Had children:
Ellen M., b. Aug. 22, 1852; Louisa J., b. Aug. 23, 1856, d. June 30, 1885; Caroline E., b. Dec. 19, 1858; Fannie B., b. Sept. 7, 1860; John R., b. May 6, 1862; F. Sumner, b. Oct. 27, 1863.

SOLON C. HOWE, son of John Howe, Sr., m. Matilda Chase. He died Jan. 9, 1885. Children:
One son who died young; Marcia M., m. Nahum S. Newton; Lucy A., m. Wm. H. Harrington.

HOLLIS HALL HOWE, b. Oct. 19, 1802, brother of Solon C. above, m. Nov. 29, 1827, Fannie Brown, daughter of Elijah Brown. Had children:
Harriet B., b. Nov. 3, 1832; Ellen F., b. July 26, 1838, m. William H. Clark.

GEORGE BUCKLEY HOWE, a brother of Hollis H., m. Had a son:
George C., who lived and died at Oakdale, leaving a widow and daughters, but no son.

THE HISTORY OF PAXTON. 115

SAMUEL HUBBARD HOWE, b. —, m. Dec. 30, 1819, Elizabeth H. Moore, d. —. Had son:
Andrew Jackson Howe, b. April 14, 1825.

ANDREW JACKSON HOWE, m. Georgiana Lakin, Feb. 2, 1858. Have no children. They reside in Cincinnati, O.

THE MAYNARDS AND PARKHURSTS.

Adam Maynard, who died here in 1786, and William, who died in 1787, are supposed to be sons of Hezekiah Maynard of Marlboro, who was the grandson of the original John Maynard of Sudbury, who came over in 1638.

MOSES MAYNARD, b. 1782–3, m. Sarah Maynard, Dec. 2, 1802. He died Feb. 12, 1857. She d. June 2, 1846. They had children:
Benjamin, b. Nov. 18, 1803; Mary, b. Aug. 20, 1805; Dolly, b. Oct. 6, 1807; Dorinda, b. June 15, 1809; Susan, b. Dec. 6, 1812.

BENJAMIN MAYNARD, m. Oct. 30, 1834, Ruth Rice, b. July 5, 1809. He died Dec. 19, 1879. She died Aug. 23, 1878. They had children:
Moses, b. Aug. 25, 1835; Solomon Rice, b. Dec. 15, 1837, d. Newport News, March 2, 1863; Ruth, b. March 16, 1846, d. May 9, 1848; Benjamin, b. Nov. 18, 1847, d. May 9, 1851; George, b. June 16, 1850, unmarried.

MOSES MAYNARD, m. Martha A. Stearns April 2, 1857. She died Oct. 2, 1876. They had children:
Benjamin L., b. Feb. 20, 1858; Charles Whitman, b. Sept. 13, 1859; William Edwin, b. Nov. 14, 1860; Joseph Henry, b. Dec. 25, 1861; Sarah Adaline, b.

Aug. 17, 1863; Ruth Rice, b. May 20, 1866; Clara Ella, b. Feb. 10, 1869; Arthur Clyde, b. June 9, 1876, died young.

BENJAMIN L. MAYNARD, m. Aug. 20, 1880, Susie P. Parkhurst, and had one child, Alice Adelle, b. Sept. 20, 1882. Mrs. Maynard is the daughter of Nathaniel L. Parkhurst, who was the son of Moses Parkhurst, who came from Petersham and m. Phebe Earle, April 7, 1819, daughter of Marmaduke Earle, and settled at the home of his father-in-law. Moses Parkhurst had children :

Nathaniel L., Varonus P., Mary E., Caroline Earle, Hiram N., and Moses B.

Benjamin L. Maynard lives in Nebraska, and has one child, Alice Adelle.

THE METCALFS.

EBENEZER METCALF came from Wrentham and lived in Rutland, (now Paxton). He had son :

SETH METCALF, who married Hannah ——, and lived where Merriam now lives. He died aged 92. He had children :

Amos, b. Feb. 14, 1785; Hannah, b. May 9, 1787, d. Nov. 24, 1795 : Seth, Jr., b. April 21, 1789, d. Dec. 10, 1795; Timothy, b. —, d. Nov. 21, 1795; Amos, b. —, d. Nov. 29, 1795; John P., b. April 21, 1791, d. —, 1884.

JOHN P. METCALF, m. Lydia Spring of Holden, about 1825. Had children :

Hannah B., b. March 31, 1827, m. William Brown; Seth, b. Nov. 28, 1828, d. young; John R., b. Jan—, 1833, m.—

HANNAH BANCROFT METCALF, m. William Brown, Nov. 24, 1852. Had son, Wesley E.

PARTRIDGE FAMILY.

TIMOTHY PARTRIDGE, m.— Lived in Medway. Had son:
Samuel, b. March 18, 1756.

SAMUEL PARTRIDGE, settled at the place now owned by Morris Kane. He married Elizabeth MacIntire. She was born Oct. 11, 1759. He died March, 29, 1832. She died Jan. 12, 1830. They had children :
Nabby, b. Nov. 14, 1782 ; Silence, b. Oct. 2, 1784 ; Zillah, b. March 27, 1786 ; Polly, b. May 11, 1789 ; Betsey, b. Nov. 11, 1791 ; David, b. March 30, 1795 ; John, b. June 1, 1797 ; Sally, b. Jan. 9, 1801.

JOHN PARTRIDGE, m. — Peirce, daughter of Job Peirce of Paxton. They had children :
George W., and several daughters.

THE MOORE FAMILY.

MARY MOORE, mother of Captain Phineas Moore, d. May 9, 1786, aged 89.

CAPT. PHINEAS MOORE, b. March —, 1729, m. Anna Rice, June 14, 1753, and died Dec. 15, 1807. His wife d. Jan. 12, 1814. The children of Phineas and Anna Moore were :
Beulah, b. May 17, 1755, d. Sept. 17, 1756 ; Relief, b. March 20, 1757 ; d. May 12, 1830 ; Pliny, b. July 15, 1759——; Beulah, b. July 29, 1761, d. June 14, 1781 ; Adonijah, b. Oct. 13, 1763, d. July 27, 1815 ; Persis, b. Aug. 29, 1766, d. Sept. 4, 1827 ; Hannah, b. Aug. 6,

1768, d. April 4, 1810; Peter, b. June 15, 1770, d. Aug. 6, 1773; Lucinda, b. July 12, 1772; Peter and Phineas, b. May 3, 1775, Peter d. June 6, 1775, Phineas d. June 17, 1775.

Captain Pliny Moore, b. about 1760, d. April 26, 1823. He married Hannah Knight, 1781. She died Nov. 9, 1809, aged 48.

Maj. Willard Moore, b. April 1743, m. March 18, 1762, to Elizabeth Hubbard; he was killed at the battle of Bunker Hill, June 17, 1776.

THE SLADE FAMILY.

Henry Slade, m. Naomi —, came from Somerset to Paxton, and had children:

John, b. Dec. 23, 1782; Anthony, b. Oct. 18, 1779; Ruth, b. March 17, 1790; Mary, b. April 2, 1792; Henry, Jr., b. July 31, 1786; Samuel, b. Aug. 28, 1794. The latter settled on what is now known as Dodd's Hill, formerly Slade's Hill, a half mile this side of the Worcester town line. He had children:
Mercy, and others.

John Slade, son of Henry, m. Lucretia ——, settled in the northerly portion of the town near the Rutland road and had children, Henry and John. The former lives near his father's place, and m. 1st, Anna Howard, May 30, 1849, and 2d, m. to Mrs. Caroline Earle Woodbury, Jan. 16, 1889, a native of this town and the daughter of Moses Parkhurst, who came from Petersham and settled in Paxton on the old Marmaduke Earle place on the Barre road. He married Phebe Earle, daughter of Marmaduke Earle. They had children:

Nathaniel L., Varonus P., Moses B., Hiram N. and Caroline Earle.

JOHN SLADE, JR., b. Feb. 3, 1827, m. Jane E. Wheeler, of Royalston, Nov. 28, 1856, and has two children :
Edgar P. Slade, b. Dec. 9, 1857, m. Mary J. Brown, Nov.—, 1886 ; Ada Idelle, b. June —, 1860.

THE SNOW FAMILY.

JOHN SNOW, b. — m. Sybil Mathews. He d. March 6, 1801, aged 72. She d. June 20, 1802, aged 69. Had children :
Daniel, m. Annie Tierney, March 31, 1787 ; James, m. Persis Warren, May 17, 1785 ; Nathan, m. Betsey Dyer, Sept. 23, 1802 ; Willard, b.——; John, b. April 27, 1772 ; Lemuel —.

COL. WILLARD SNOW, b. —, d. July 13, 1846, m. 1st, Polly Harrington, daughter of Dea. Samuel Harrington, m. 2d, Sarah Davis, sister of "Honest John Davis." Children by 1st wife were :
Polly ; Lucy, b. March 23, 1805 ; Sophronia, b. Jan. 7. 1808 ; Sybil, b. May 13, 1818 ; Carlo Homer, b. Nov. 11, ——; d. about 1830 ; John, b. Oct. 30, 1801, d. Jan. 15, 1828 ; Willard, b. —; Henry, by 2d wife. He lives near Newton.

CARLO HOMER SNOW, m. Delia Newton, daughter of Windsor Newton. Had children :
Windsor Newton, b. March 24, 1824 ; Carlo Homer, b. — .

DR. WINDSOR N. SNOW, m. Julia F. Wright of Grafton, May 10, 1854. He resides in Worcester and has children :
Ida, Florence, Homer, Wallace. Miss Florence is

a graduate of Smith's College, and Wallace is at Harvard University.

CARLO HOMER SNOW, m. Lucretia Eddy. They had Nelson H., who is living at Mineral Point, Wis.

WILLARD SNOW, 2d, m. Mary Peirce, Oct. 28, 1818.

The Snow family were among the most prominent of the early settlers. They were men of fine presence, tall and portly. Col. Willard Snow was over six feet in height, and towards the last of his life, weighed over three hundred pounds. He built 28 houses in Paxton. All of his male descendants are distinguished looking men. His mother was sitting in the doorway one morning when suddenly a bear and two cubs passed through the yard and into the woods.

THE WARREN FAMILY.

JOHN WARREN,[1] came to Watertown in 1630, at the age of 45. He d. Dec. 13. 1667. Had one son, viz:

JOHN WARREN, JR.,[2] b. 1622, and died in 1703.

JOHN WARREN,[3] 3d., b. May 21, 1678, d. 1726 at Weston. Had son.

JOHN WARREN,[4] b. April 3, 1701, settled in Marlboro; d. Dec. 27, 1783. Had son.

JOHN WARREN,[4] b. June 19, 1739. He d. May 1, 1812, aged 73, m. Rachel —. She died Feb. 23, 1709, aged 69. He died aged 94 years and 8 months. Had children:

Anna, b. Dec. 15, 1766; Rachel, b. Jan. 27, 1772; Lydia, b. March 15, 1774; Lavinia, b. Sept. 4, 1778.

WILLIAM WARREN,[5] b. in Marlboro, May 13, 1769, m. Amey Eddy, 1791, d. Jan. 13, 1864. Had children:

Abigail, b. July 12, 1792 ; Phebe, b. May 14, 1794 ; John, b. March 18, 1797.

JOHN WARREN, [6] b. March 18, 1797, m. March 24, 1824, Lucretia Mirick, b. Jan. 25, 1803. Had children ;
Mary Ann Condy, b. July 30, 1825, m. Sept. 12, 1843, Jonathan Hapgood ; Sewell Mirick, b. Nov. 28, 1826, d. Nov. 21, 1828 ; Anna Eddy, b. Dec. 12, 1828 ; William Mirick, b. Sept. 17, 1832 ; Persis Graves, b. Dec. 10, 1834 ; Bezaleel Mirick, b. Dec. 28, 1836, d. Feb. 19, 1837 ; Phebe Elizabeth, b. Nov. 30, 1837 ; George Harrison, b. March 28, 1840 ; Ellen Lucretia, b. April 4, 1842 ; Harriet Maria, b. Dec. 24, 1844, d. Oct. 1, 1844.

ANNA E. WARREN, [7] m. John S. Chase, Oct. 9, 1845. They had children :
Wallace S., b. June 28, 1847 ; Charles E., b. Nov. 14, 1849, d. Aug. 26, 1870 ; Emmons W., b. Feb. 17, 1854 ; Carrie E., b. Aug. 25, 1856 ; Emma, b. Oct. 18, 1859, d. Feb. 9, 1877 ; George Harrison, b. Aug. 2, 1865, d. March 21, 1866.

WILLIAM M. WARREN, [8] son of John Warren above, m. 1st, Mary Hale Bowen, June 11, 1856. Had children :
Anna Lucretia, b. Aug. 29, 1860, d. Sept. 4, 1864 ; Anna Maria, b. April 18, 1865, d. March 17, 1884 ; Arthur Luther, b. June 27, 1866, d. Sept. 15, 1867. Mrs. Mary H. Warren, d. April 18, 1874.

He married 2d, Susan Catharine Woodbury, Feb. 9, 1876. Had :
John Lovell, b. Jan. 19, 1882, d. March 28, 1886.

www.ingramcontent.com/pod-product-compliance
Lightning Source LLC
Chambersburg PA
CBHW022141160426
43197CB00009B/1383